THE BIG
MINI BOOK

THE BIG
MINI BOOK

Johannes Hübner

BAY VIEW BOOKS

Published 1992 by
Bay View Books Ltd
13a Bridgeland Street
Bideford, Devon EX39 2QE

© Copyright HEEL-Verlag GmbH 1989
English translation © Copyright Bay
View Books Ltd 1992

Typesetting and layout by Chris Fayers

ISBN 1 870979 21 4
Printed in Hong Kong

Contents

Mr MINI – Sir Alec Issigonis

There is no question that the Mini is one of the most ingenious designs created since the Second World War: a vehicle that was not only ten years ahead of its time, but a concept that established a formula as valid today as in 1960. Indeed, most modern cars – and not just the small ones – follow this formula.

What sort of a man conceived this small marvel? Alec Issigonis came from a well-to-do cosmopolitan family and even as a child travelled with his family all over Europe. He was born on 18th November 1906, the son of an exiled Greek of British nationality, living with his Bavarian wife in what is now Izmir. Shipbuilding in the Ottoman empire provided a splendid living for the shipyard engineer, but in 1922 the Turks repossessed their land in Greek hands and forced all Christians to flee. British nationals were evacuated by the Royal Navy but the affair caused Alec's father such a shock that he died en route in Malta.

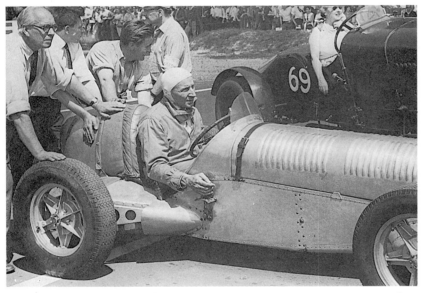

Alec Issigonis at the wheel of the Lightweight Special at a historic meeting at Oulton Park. George Dowson is behind the right rear wheel.

The Mini's designer at the Birmingham International Motor Show with Lord Snowdon, his friend and supporter.

Mrs Issigonis, now widowed, arrived with her 16 year old son in her adopted homeland – fortunately with a decent pension. Young Alec was meant to go to art college, for even when he was a little boy he showed a talent for drawing, but his fascination with matters technical led him to enrol at the well-known Battersea Polytechnic. However he failed his exams for lack of mathematical knowledge, and entry to university was closed to him. Nothing daunted, Alec and his mother acquired a Weymann-bodied Singer and toured Europe to have a look at car manufacturing plants and mechanical engineering works.

Back in London Alec met Edward Gillet, who had a design studio in Victoria Road. An agreement was reached jointly to develop an automatic clutch. It was meant to be a precursor of the automatic gearbox, working by manifold depression. The clutch was meant to operate automatically when opening or shutting the throttle butterfly valve – both Humber and Rover showed interest, and even Chrysler knocked at Gillet's door. This reputation resulted in Issigonis moving to Humber in 1934 as a technical draughtsman. Here, among other projects, he helped to overcome the early problems of independent front suspension.

At the same time he worked with his friend George Dowson at his hobby: the development of a potent racing car for sprints and hill-climbs, such as the famous Shelsley Walsh.

It was the middle of 1938 before the Lightweight Special was ready for competition – in the meantime Issigonis had moved to Morris at Cowley, still working on independent suspensions. The Lightweight possessed rubber suspension, only weighed 1100lbs (500kg) and was considered, as John Bolster said in his 1949 book *Specials*, 'one of the most beautiful specials of British origin'.

It had a plywood chassis frame strengthened by aluminium body panels. The front suspension was independent and built on the dining room table at home. A blown Austin 750cc racing engine delivered almost 60bhp at the flywheel, making the car particularly quick off the mark. The car continued to race during the war and in 1947 they developed a new overhead cam 750cc engine. Ultimately, however, Issigonis decided that racing cars did not provide solutions that could be applied to series production vehicles.

But back to 1936: the 30-year old Issigonis was now in the Morris engineering department and working on an independent front suspension system using coil springs and unequal length wishbones. He added rack-and-pinion steering and this was fitted to the new MG Y-type and much later was even used on the MGB.

Issigonis' real fame came with with a production car that at the time was a sensation in Britain, the Morris Minor,

Sir Alec, practical engineer *par excellence*.

clearly bearing its creator's imprint. The first plans emerged during the war: Issigonis visualized front suspension by longitudinal torsion bars and a unit-construction, stress-bearing, pressed steel body.

With hindsight, the Morris Minor is as much of a landmark as the later Mini. It was built in various forms from October 1948 until February 1972. It pioneered the modern small car, offering excellent roadholding and reasonable comfort for four people, who were transported at low cost and acceptable speeds. In 23 years production exceeded 1.6 million vehicles.

The torsion bar front suspension was not the only item to show the way forward – he also used 14in wheels when everyone swore by 15in or even 16in sizes. There is an interesting story about the last experimental car, which seemed to Issigonis simply too narrow and tall. When its creator looked critically at it, the idea occurred to him to cut it right through along the centre line and widen it by 4in. No sooner said than done, and it was in that widened form that the car was put into production. A flat-four engine was abandoned during development, and the old 918cc side-valve engine dating back to the pre-war Morris 8 was pressed into service, to be replaced in 1952 by the more modern pushrod 803cc unit which powered the Austin A30. 948cc and 1098cc versions followed.

The marriage between Austin and Morris in 1952 to form BMC presented Issigonis with a new management opposed to many of his ideas, for instance front-wheel drive for the Minor. Consolidation rather than investment was the watchword, profits came first.

The Morris Minor combined independent front suspension by torsion bars and rack-and-pinion steering, giving excellent road manners for the day.

On 26th August 1959 at the British Army proving grounds in Surrey, Issigonis presented a fleet of the first Austin Sevens and Morris Mini Minors to the international press.

Issigonis left BMC and turned to another manufacturer, who offered more interesting prospects than just the control of production budgets. He joined Alvis in Coventry, makers of quality sporting cars and with a fine old name in the British motor industry.

His brief was to build a new high-performance car to replace the slightly outdated Alvis 3-litre. At Alvis Issigonis met Chris Kingham, a gifted engine designer. Jointly they built a 3.5-litre twin-cam V8, and this engine was to be incorporated in a monocoque body/chassis together with a new transmission.

Back in the 1920s Issigonis had designed a two-speed transmission operated by two pedals like the Ford Model T. This was backed up by a normal, electrically operated overdrive, so that the driver, in effect, had four speeds available. Issigonis redesigned this system for the Alvis sports saloon to eliminate clutch operation after the car had moved off. History has it that he wanted to fit the overdrive next to the rear axle to reduce the size of the transmission tunnel and to improve weight distribution – a sort of transaxle of the fifties.

The suspension was also new. He turned to his old friend Alex Moulton, who later designed the Hydrolastic suspension for the Mini and other BMC models. For the Alvis, Moulton designed a hydraulically coupled front and rear suspension which accepted all the suspension forces in one central unit.

Issigonis was very keen on this concept, but Alvis took fright at the high tooling costs required for such a revolutionary vehicle. For Alvis, car production was a secondary matter – their main concerns were building military vehicles and aircraft engines. After much discussion, it was decided not to build the Alvis dream car,

but rather to go for the new 14-cylinder radial aero-engine intended to power the future Westland Whirlwind helicopter. Before Issigonis had time to reflect on his wasted four years, Sir Leonard Lord called him back to Austin at Longbridge in 1956, there to take charge, in the so-called Kremlin, of the advanced engineering design office. Sir Leonard also wanted something entirely new, but practical, cheap and successful. From Alvis, Issigonis brought the idea of integrated suspensions, remote transmission and something like half an Alvis V8 engine – in other words the new Austin was to be powered by a 1500cc light-alloy engine with an overhead camshaft. This was during a troubled period for the United Kingdom, when the Suez canal was closed as Egypt's dictator Gamal Abdel Nasser demonstrated his power to the western world. This caused fuel rationing at the rate of some four gallons per month for motorists and resulted in a flood of underpowered small 'bubble' cars, mostly of German origin.

Lord responded by throwing out Issigonis' project and demanded designs for a new small car. What eventually emerged was the Mini, and that was to become a worldwide sensation.

The Mini was the foundation stone of a successful formula, which many of today's cars of much greater size and power follow: take a transverse engine, combine it with a compact gearbox, add a differential and power the front wheels. At BMC, Issigonis' ideas were further developed and in 1962 the four-door 1100 with the BMC 1098cc A-series engine came into being. At first, 48bhp at 5100 rpm was available, but later it was available with the 1275cc engine as the 1300. There was a GT version in 1970, but this was still not the end for the Hydrolastic suspension first seen in 1962 on the 1100. Predictably, the 1100 was not only available in Austin and Morris guises, but also as Riley, MG, Vanden Plas and Wolseley.

The end of 1964 saw the debut of the 1800, which looked like a longer and rounder 1100. Interior space in the 1800 exceeded that of the then current Mercedes and Jaguar. Under the bonnet was a new version of the B-series engine, producing 87bhp from 1798cc, but it still had a side-camshaft and a long stroke. The car could exceed 90mph and as standard equipment had two-speed wipers, reclining seats, heated rear screen and a light in the boot.

The 1800 led on a little later to the five-door Maxi – big brother to the Mini; its 1500cc engine had an overhead camshaft and was later bored out to 1748cc.

A 'Mini successor', the 9X, was as ingenious as the original Mini. Issigonis laid it out around a slender ohc 1.3-litre engine and while it was to have been slightly shorter than the Mini it would have been roomier. This was his last complete car design for BMC, and it was abandoned in favour of a cheaper policy of revised models.

A party was given to mark his well-deserved retirement in 1971. By way of background decoration, Timo Makinen's Monte Carlo winning Mini AJB 44B was there, flanked by one of the first Minis, the first Minor, an 1100 and an 1800. So the great designer was pensioned off.

In the meantime he had been knighted and had become a Fellow of the Royal Society. This prompted him to say that he felt it had too many academic members and that a

The Maxi was characterized by maximum provision of interior space within its overall dimensions but its looks lacked the Mini's appeal.

The Austin 1300, more powerful sister of the 1100. This range saw the first use of Hydrolastic suspension.

simple 'ironmonger' like him would serve as something of a counterbalance to them – honest words from one who always thought of himself as an artist and who considered mathematics as the enemy of really creative people. He revolutionized the automobile world, creating design criteria on which cars are still being built today.

Even after retirement, Sir Alec continued to work for BL and later Austin Rover as a consultant. He maintained an office at Longbridge, where a secretary dealt with his still sizeable postbag, containing letters from Mini enthusiasts world-wide. Two mechanics were kept busy in a small workshop translating the master's ideas into practice, and when Sir Alec became too infirm to drive to the factory, liaison engineer Rodney Bull would visit him at his home on an almost daily basis. Mark Snowdon, sometime head of Austin Rover product planning, befriended Sir Alec and solicited his opinion on current company projects.

One favourite project was a steam-engined car. Another was the gearless Mini which had no gearbox or clutch, just a torque converter built in unit with the final drive and simple forward/reverse gears, controlled by a three-position lever on the facia. The car had coil spring suspension and the ohc engine from project 9X. It would have needed considerable development, as it was too thirsty and its acceleration too leisurely – but a prototype served Sir Alec well for commuting in Birmingham. Work on the 9X engine continued, a fascinating development being the six-cylinder version which was installed in an MG Metro. Luckily this prototype has been preserved for posterity along with examples of the gearless Minis, now kept in the Heritage Museum.

For many years Sir Alec continued to enjoy the limelight of public attention, and could always be relied upon to come up with a few good quotes for his contacts in the media – especially if they took the trouble to ask him out for a decent lunch in a favourite restaurant. But his health gradually deteriorated. He contracted Parkinson's disease, and became more and more of a recluse. He gave up his house in Birmingham's Edgbaston suburb – with the house went his large model railway layout, which ran through both house and garden – and he also gave up another passion, for Meccano engineering sets. His specially requested retirement present from colleagues had been the largest Meccano set available...

Sir Alec moved into a small ground floor flat, the unmarried man living alone after his mother's death many years before, until the end. His flat was curiously impersonal, reflecting perhaps that he felt above his surroundings and other material concerns. He retained very few close personal friends, and in his solitude was prone to bouts of depression, not helped by his illness. One of few passions that remained was his liking for classic American detective fiction, which he read and re-read in old dog-eared paperback editions.

He died on 2nd October 1988, a few weeks short of his 82nd birthday. At his funeral and at the memorial service held a few weeks later, old friends and colleagues gathered to pay their last respects – Alex Moulton, Jack Daniels, Chris Kingham, Charles Griffin and others. The Earl of Snowdon read the address at the memorial service in Birmingham Cathedral, while the first Morris Minor and the first Mini-Minor were parked outside.

On Christopher Wren's tomb in St Paul's Cathedral are engraved the words 'Si Monumentum Requiris, Circumspice'. To see Sir Alec Issigonis' memorial, we have to look no further than the next Mini we meet on the road...

Alec Issigonis' farewell party in 1971: here we see him next to Mini Number 1. On the left is the first Morris Minor, on the right the 1965 Monte winner driven by Makinen/Easter, but with the wrong Mk II grille. Behind 621AOK hides an 1100 and at the back there is a big 1800.

MINI Beginnings: From Prototypes to Production Cars

What Leonard Lord wanted was a practical small car which was to offer the maximum interior space for the minimum external size while making very economical use of materials. It was to be 'bigger than it looked', and existing technology could not provide the solution. Issigonis set to, and it was about this time that he started his custom of inviting his collaborators to a restaurant for informal chats, a custom he continued with a wider circle when he was later joined by John Cooper and Daniel Richmond (of Downton Engineering).

In early 1957 Issigonis was joined by his friend from Alvis, the engine man Chris Kingham, and Jack Daniels from Morris, who shared Alec's enthusiasm for new suspension systems. Many a menu, envelope back and even tablecloth were covered with drawings, ideas and calculations – then taken to Longbridge where prototype development under John Sheppard and Vic Everton was planned. In this way Issigonis created a sketchbook which set out his ideas for the design office.

An overall vehicle length of only 10ft left the designers 24in within which to fit the engine/transmission unit. Lord's instruction that only an engine from BMC's series production could be used left only the A series four-cylinder as a viable possibility. But that engine measured 38in from radiator to gearbox output shaft. They tried to shorten it by eliminating two cylinders but this idea was given up after testing proved it unsatisfactory.

Then a sketch came up which pointed the way towards a technical solution to the space problem: under the outline of a Morris Minor with a modernised semi-monocoque body was a transverse-mounted rearward-inclined four-cylinder engine, with oil sump containing the gearbox and differential. The fan was to be driven by gears from the overhead camshaft. Issigonis said later that he had carried that idea in his head for a long time and drawn it at the right, lucky moment. To all involved in the project, this was the moment of revelation. Chris Kingham hurriedly tested whether, contrary to all belief, the gearbox and differential could manage without the customary lubricant and run in engine oil. There were just seven months left to try this out. The fact is that Leonard Lord was able to try the prototype in July 1958 and after all of five minutes made up his mind and ordered that the car had to be ready for production within twelve months. A lot was left to be done...

The A series engine in its original 803cc form powered the Series II Morris Minor and the Austin A30. At the time when the Mini project was being worked on a 948cc version had been developed, to be used in the Minor 1000 and Austin A35. The fact that the A series unit has remained in production for more than 40 years is proof of the soundness of the original design. It had a cast iron block and head, and a side camshaft operating overhead valves via pushrods. The crankshaft drove the camshaft via a

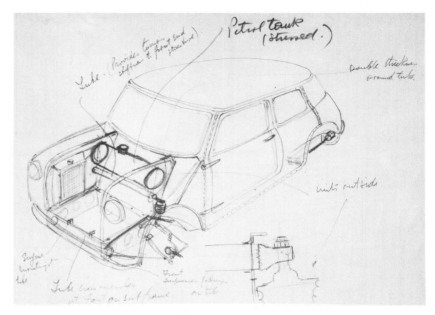

Original drawing by Issigonis: radiator on right, fuel tank in engine bay and sketches of suspension system.

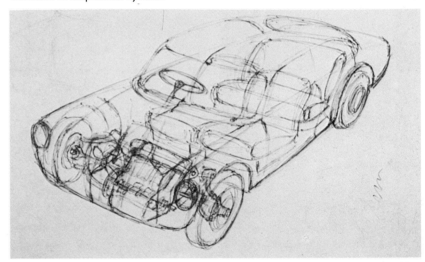

This sketch shows a body similar to the Minor with an overhead cam engine inclined to the rear; the camshaft drives the fan via gearing.

roller-chain, the oil pump was driven from the rear end of the camshaft and, at the other end, the water pump and generator were driven by a vee-belt. When bored out to 948cc the crank journals and bearings were widened and a full-flow oil filter added. The first prototype, fitted with a 948cc engine, pushed out 37bhp and exceeded 85mph with a single SU carburettor. In the Mini a 1¼in SU unit was used and this engine was fitted to prototype XC9003, also known as the Orange Box. It was installed with the inlet and carburettor facing forward, but after the first tests the whole power unit was rotated by 180 degrees because problems arose with carburettor icing and poor running due to too cold a mixture.

However, Chris Kingham's men thought it dangerous to expose John Q. Customer to a car only 10ft long, weighing

A 1958 pre-production 948cc engine from the driver's side, including the subframe. The serial number 950 on the engine block (left), signifies the cubic capacity, MOWOG was the Morris and BMC parts trade mark, the gear lever is attached to the short gearshaft and the rubber suspension units can be seen. This engine was reduced to 848cc because it was considered too powerful.

Under the bonnet of the Orange Box with its A35 grille sits the future Mini engine with exhaust and carburettor still in front. The battery is on the right and on the left can be seen the water hose leading to the radiator in the wing. Later the engine was turned through 180 degrees. The one-piece bonnet and grille could not be used for reasons of rigidity.

Grille apart, this styling sketch is very similar to the production car.

600kg, with a 37bhp engine and capable of some 85mph. It was then decided to reduce cubic capacity by exactly 100cc, it being too costly to develop more powerful brakes within the 10in rims.

Unfortunately it had been overlooked that rotating the engine meant placing the distributor and coil right behind the grille. This meant that in heavy rain, sooner or later the engine stopped working.

Mini waterproofing was inadequate partly because the summer of 1959 was warm and dry. Thus during tests no one noticed that a stiffening rib was unhappily positioned, with the result that water collected and the distributor and coil were exposed to water spray. Customers noticed when their new Minis stopped in the rain. A special water test was set up by BMC and the position of the stiffening rib was altered in production, but ignition problems are familiar to Mini drivers even today.

For the 1986 model year Austin Rover introduced a cover, fitted between grille and engine, to divert the water. The Clubman version had this already in 1969.

Turning the A series engine round caused an additional problem for Kingham and his colleagues – there was need for an extra gear in the box; otherwise Mini drivers would have had one forward and four reverse speeds!

The additional gear introduced to alter the rotational direction produced noise; this was acceptable to the technicians because the gearbox modifications enabled a reduction in engine revolutions, which in its turn lessened crankshaft loading. Engine testbed measurements revealed that critical vibration was now outside the rev limits of the little four cylinder unit. Kingham's team reduced cubic capacity by shortening the stroke from 73.7 to 68.2mm, the bore remaining the same. Maximum power of 34bhp (net) was now produced at 5500rpm. Maximum torque of 44lb/ft came at 2900rpm. Turning the engine around under the bonnet not only changed the position of the radiator but also the way it worked. In the old arrangement the fan used a lot of power to suck in relatively little air from the low pressure area within the wing and simultaneously sucked dirt and water into the engine compartment. When the radiator position was changed, the fan blades were reversed and hot air from the radiator was expelled into the wing.

Installing the gears and differential in the sump necessitated siting the clutch outboard. It proved difficult to cope with the problem of sealing. Road testing revealed again and again that oil from the engine/gearbox penetrated into the clutch, leading to clutch slip and ultimate failure. John Sheppard and Vic Everton eventually found a solution to this problem.

The gearchange on the first test cars was operated by the 'pull-and-push' system as on the Citroën 2CV, DKW and Renault 4 – the lever stuck out like a walking stick through the dash below the screen. But the gears were difficult to find and the lever's imprecise action was made worse when the engine was turned through 180 degrees, for it then became necessary to run the linkage through the sump. Pre-production cars got a normal central gearlever, without the through-the-sump linkage.

Engine bay of an 850 Super de Luxe with sound-deadening material, separate hydraulic fluid reservoirs and the wiper motor at right hand top.

For the driveshafts universal joints were required which needed no maintenance and were robust, as well as being cheap and simple to manufacture. At GKN they remembered the Rzeppa constant velocity joints, known since 1926. GKN bought the licence rights from Unipower and set today's trend for the manufacture of driveshaft joints – used now by most manufacturers of front-drive vehicles. Charles Griffin and Jack Daniels set about adapting the classically simple Rzeppa joints to the requirements of the new car. With the collaboration of GKN the constant-velocity joints they evolved gave great reliability and 40 degrees of wheel movement. Simple Hooke joints were used at the inner ends of the driveshafts.

Jack Daniels, the chassis man, designed a front suspension layout very similar to the Morris Minor. Above and below the driveshafts there was a cast suspension arm, the lower one located by a rubber-mounted tie-rod. A rack-and-pinion steering system had been fitted to the Minor and this was modified for the Mini.

For the suspension, Issigonis and Moulton had conceived an all-independent system: rubber, instead of torsion bars or steel springs, was to be the medium.

Rubber was cheap and practical for a light car with a high payload. Calculations were based on a dry weight of 600kg but a total overall weight of almost a tonne – after all the future Austin 'Newmarket' was meant for four people and luggage.

Surprisingly, Leonard Lord approved of the plan to use rubber suspension. It would save space and be light and cheap. Picture the suspension like this: a cone is attached to the suspension arm, with an inverted cone above it. So that the two cones do not touch, the top cone is joined to the bottom one by strong rubber bellows. This rubber unit, together with the air between the two cones and a shock absorber, jointly took care of the car's suspension. At the front, these suspension units were fitted vertically, but at the rear were installed within the subframe. The rear shock absorbers were attached to the trailing arms directly behind the hubs and to the inner wings. When tested on the Orange Box this system's practicability was established and it only needed fine tuning. The battery and fuel tank had to be moved to the rear, because it was found that on braking the rear wheels were insufficiently loaded and locked up too easily. A brake limiter was also fitted. On top of this, testing established that front and rear

Power unit without subframe and manifolds but with drive shafts, demonstrating the revolutionary compactness of the engine/transmission unit. Remote gearchange came to all Minis in 1973, though Coopers had it earlier.

Rear subframe of a late 1980s Mini with six-point attachment.

subframes were absolutely necessary. When comparing two test cars, where suspension members were bolted direct to the body, even short drives showed up considerable fatigue. Sound deadening, and the prevention of vibration being transmitted to the body, received careful consideration. The subframes later turned out to be ideal for fitting to special bodies of all sorts, for engine and transmission could be attached on its subframe to any desired chassis and the rear subframe made it possible to choose any length of wheelbase. Small firms using plastics bodywork and tubular chassis created often very attractive and original vehicles, using the subframes. Originally Issigonis planned to connect the rear wheels by a light tube, to maintain constant camber and track. But using a rigid axle tube would have meant raising the rear floor and finding room for the exhaust above this axle. Because of this Issigonis and Daniels abandoned the idea and went for reinforcement of the rear suspension arm mountings instead. The only small alteration was a slight toe-in of the rear wheels, whilst the fronts had a slight toe-out. This set-up ensured superb straight running and compensated for any oversteer tendency. This is the small secret which lies behind the Mini's swervability.

Using 10in wheels meant breaking new ground and for a while the BMC technicians insisted that such a wheel size would cause the Mini to 'fall into every manhole'. Yet these small wheels helped give the Mini its astonishing roominess, and road testing demonstrated that the problems did not lie with the wheels but with the brakes. There was only room for 7in brake drums within the rims; enough for the rear but barely adequate for the front. John Cooper later solved this problem and for his sporting versions developed disc brakes in collaboration with Lockheed. For the series production car the same company devised a brake equalizer, preventing excessive hydraulic pressure at the rear and transferring it to the front.

Traversing a water splash on the test circuit became part of the test programme after early complaints of wet feet and drowned ignition.

From Orange Box to Mini

It says something for Issigonis' far-sightedness and genius that the car he first conceived – monocoque construction, front and rear subframes, transverse engine and side radiator – was the car the public finally got, but he still had some way to go to its complete realization.

The first project, XC9001, was a four-door saloon and had 13in wheels. It was carried through as far as the making of a running prototype. This was set aside until it was used as a basis for the 1800, which appeared in 1964. XC9002 was clearly smaller but still had four doors. The decision was then taken to go back to one of Issigonis' first projects – the small two-door version.

Issigonis' first sketches provided such good packaging for the passenger compartment that it was incorporated practically unchanged in the series-production vehicle. But the front and rear ends went through many changes. XC9003 already had the characteristic welding seam down to the wheel arch and the sliding windows in the doors. Since the wings functioned as load bearing parts of the structure, Dick Gallimore, the body specialist, had foreseen external door hinges; similar hinges were used for the bonnet and bootlid. The first road-ready test vehicles were orange with a black roof and were nicknamed Orange Box. Evolved from XC9003, they had an A35 grille to prevent identification during test runs, which mainly took place at night. With the A35 grille fitted, the bonnet aperture began at bumper level, providing excellent engine bay access. The monocoque body received a reinforcing frame behind the rear seats – this made the car very stiff torsionally, but also very prone to rusting in that area. Issigonis avoided double skinning wherever possible, and, for reasons of rigidity, later reverted to a frame connecting the front wings. This reduced accessibility to the engine, but the Mini is built in almost the same manner to this day.

For a 1959 car the Mini had remarkably thin roof pillars and a large glass area. Inconspicuous details ensured sufficient stiffness: the roof had all-round guttering and pronounced flanges ran down the screen pillars into the wings. Under the window line ran a sharp feature line, and the rounded rear quarter panels were very rigid. The characteristic flange at the bottom of the body also increased rigidity. To this day the main-line Mini does not have fibreglass front wings, because these would considerably reduce the monocoque's strength. However, fibreglass bodies were produced in Chile in the 1960s and Facorca in Venezuela undertook a Mini lookalike body in fibreglass on Mini mechanical elements in 1991.

The sliding windows were fitted not purely for economy's sake but because Issigonis wanted maximum interior width; they only gave way to the wind-down kind on the Mark III. The hollowed-out doors formed pockets for the everyday things a driver needs. Another victim of economy were the inner door handles: these were replaced by a pull-cord running the length of the door which operated the lock mechanism. Even this had its advantages: one could neither catch in them nor injure oneself. Handles were later fitted and these brought disadvantages. Only after introducing proper door panels, window winding handles and front-mounted door

The smallest disc brake in the world, here on one of the first Coopers. Lockheed later modified this design considerably.

handles, did this nuisance disappear – but the practical door pockets had to go too.

The interior equipment of BMC's new minicar was very spartan to begin with. The purchaser did not even get a carpet on the standard model but had to make do with rubber mats, re-reinforced where the driver's heels caused maximum wear. As was typical of British car manufacturers at the time, the heater was an extra-cost option. The de Luxe model had two-tone seats and it had

Standard Mini with rubber mats, no heater, and cloth rather than two-tone vinyl seats. Note the floor-mounted starter button. We have to assume that a driver's seat was not an extra...

15

The similarity of this prototype to the later 1100 and 1800 is not only external: project XC9001 also had Hydrolastic suspension and four doors, but the ohc engine was intended to power the rear wheels.

Rear of XC9001 shows strong similarity to Mini. Note rear lights and wide rear screen pillars.

carpets. The simple switchgear and centrally mounted combination instrument of the Austin Seven/Morris Mini-Minor enabled easy production of left-hand or right-hand drive cars on the same assembly line. The starter button mounted on the floor on the right of the tunnel retained this position on left-hand drive cars so a passenger in one of these export models could, at the driver's request, operate the starter...

While testing the new car, BMC built production lines at Longbridge and Cowley which lay fallow for some time until the Mini went into production in its final form. Final meant the 848cc engine with 34.5bhp at 5500rpm and a near semi-circular radiator grille, whose top edge met the bonnet. The Austin Seven – Se7en in its early days – had outside door hinges, sliding windows but no carpets or heating – these were for the de Luxe. The car was now 10ft (3.05m) long, 55in (1397mm) wide and 53in (1346mm) high. Dry it weighed 1380lbs (626kg) and gross vehicle weight was not to exceed 2000lbs (910kg). Top speed was around 72mph (116km/h)and there were a number of cunning details. For instance, opening the boot lid downward lowered the number plate vertically and allowed extra luggage to be carried. All in all, development of the Austin Seven/Morris Mini-Minor had only taken 15 months. This record in the history of the automobile is impressive, for in this short time not just another car, but a revolutionary, pace-setting and world-beating car was developed, which survives today and has been imitated by many manufacturers of cars large and small.

▼ This sectioned Morris Mini-Minor was exhibited at the London Motor Show. Today it is in the Heritage Motor Museum.

Long-bonneted prototype XC9002 alongside a Morris Minor, showing increase in passenger space.

XC9003, well on the way to the looks of the production Mini, with only a few revisions to go.

Inside the 850 de Luxe – carpets and two-tone seats provide at least some appearance of comfort while the instrument binnacle looks lonesome on the parcels shelf.

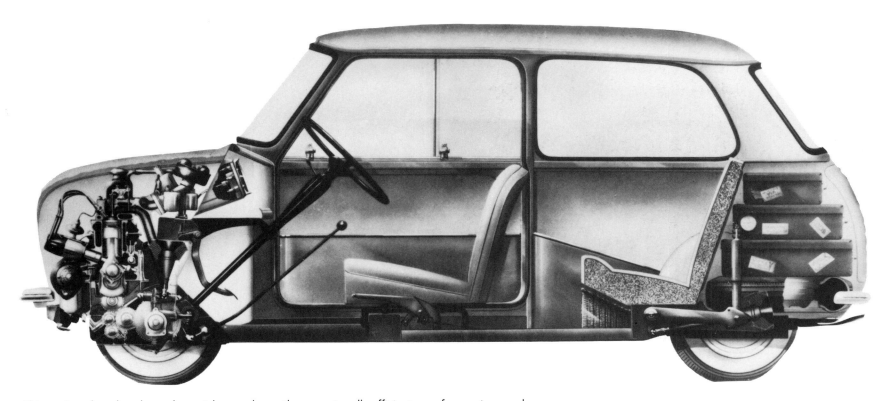

This sectioned car has the early straight gear lever. The exceptionally efficient use of space is very clear.

17

MINI Grows Up

The Morris Mini/Austin Seven was conceived as a no-frills vehicle but, not surprisingly, many customers wanted a luxurious version and in September 1961 Super versions were announced, just a few months before the Austin-badged cars were also named Mini. Externally the Supers could be recognized by two-tone paint schemes and new grilles. Inside there were door handles instead of pull cords, carpets in the luggage compartment and on the floor. Elaborate sound-deadening was complemented by a 16-blade fan which gave such a different engine sound that it was adopted for the whole model range. Lessons learned through racing meant stronger rims on the wheels, which now had all-over chrome trims. Drivers benefited from key starting, instead of having to prod the floor button.

BMC were never shy about badge-engineering, and in October 1961 the Riley Elf and Wolseley Hornet were introduced simultaneously. Outwardly they were immediately recognizable by vertical radiator grilles and extended boots. Both acquired new bonnets, fitted with Wolseley or Riley grilles, having additional small horizontal air intakes with built-in sidelights – all of which gave the Mini a totally different aspect. The vertical centre grille opened with the bonnet. Both these luxury Minis had heftier bumper blades and overriders, and the rear quarter welding seam ended at the waist line, allowing for miniscule fins to

The Morris Super, from August 1961, had extra nudge bars for the bumpers and two-tone paint. The grille had seven vertical decorative bars.

balance the boot lines. The boot compartment was 10in (25cm) longer, providing a lot more luggage room than the Mini, and the boot lid was top hinged.

Inside, the Elf had a full-width wooden dash, whilst in the Hornet a wooden surround to the oval instrument cluster

Wolseley Hornet Series III with hidden door hinges and winding windows. Its radiator grille badge was illuminated, according to a Wolseley tradition.

This picture clearly shows the grille variations: Mini Super, Minivan, Austin de Luxe and Cooper.

sufficed. This was not the only reason for a slightly higher price for the Elf: different door trims and a chromed gear lever distinguished the Elf from the Hornet. Weight had increased from 1380lbs (626kg) to 1477lbs (670kg); this obviously meant less performance. Both models had better padded seats than the Mini, with a combination of cloth and leather upholstery. In 1963 a 998cc engine with 40bhp was introduced. At first this was only available in the Elf and Hornet, but because of its entirely different block it offered much better tuning possibilities than the Mini engine, and it became available from January 1964 for the Cooper. At first sight, increasing the Cooper's capacity from 997cc to 998cc seemed pointless, but it made sense because the bore/stroke ratios of the engines were very different. A bore of 64.58mm and stroke of 76.2mm on the Riley compared with 62.43 and 81.28 on the original Cooper, which meant considerably higher piston speeds. This apart, the Riley achieved maximum torque of 52lb/ft at only 2700rpm, while the Cooper's 997cc engine was rated at 54lb/ft at 3600rpm and the 998cc 9FD engine had 57lb/ft at 3000rpm.

The Mini was under continuous development. From

The Wolseley's dash was rather less impressive than the Riley's.

January 1962 the brake wheel cylinders were enlarged, seat coverings were improved and the de Luxe and Super combined to become the Super de Luxe. An estate car, known as the Austin Seven Countryman or Morris Mini-Traveller, had been launched in 1960 with wood trim to the body, and now became available also without the wood trim. The original 'Seven' name for the little 850, so named after the successful 'Seven' of pre-war years and used since the start of production, was dropped in favour of 'Mini' from January 1962.

As early as 1961 BMC had had to fit a strengthened gearbox because of an increasing number of complaints about the earlier unit, which largely consisted of A35 parts. The synchromesh proved too weak, an effect of an increased number of gear wheels rotating in engine oil rather than gear oil, and second gear had a habit of failing. It also became apparent that in day-to-day use the old clutch sealing problems raised their head again. A new type of oil seal was found, slightly more expensive but capable of remaining oil-tight without lubrication. This Deva seal saved BMC many thousands of pounds in expensive warranty repairs.

In early 1963, the Riley Elf and Wolseley Hornet were given the 998cc engine and received wider front brakes with two leading shoes to cope with their higher performance. All Austin/Morris models received improvements, including a 10% reduction of the wiped area of the screen, because the wipers until then had swept right to the edge of the screen, trapping moisture and causing rot.

The rally experiences of 1964 brought about more re-working and strengthening of the gearbox, with an overall reduction in friction generated by its revolving parts. Previously this had caused catastrophic failures due to the oil overheating. The gear train was revised in such a way that fewer but larger and thicker gear teeth achieved the same gearing as before. The second and third gear mainshaft now revolved in needle rollers and the layshaft in a roller cage to prevent axial misalignment. The selector forks were replaced by bigger ones with larger bearing surfaces and the new gearbox

Tightly-packaged gearbox.

◀ This is the Riley Elf Mark III, with full-width veneered dash, three instruments, two glove boxes, and swivelling face-level air vents.

At the rear the only differences between the Wolseley Hornet and the Riley Elf were the badges. These cars always had overriders at the back and the bigger rear screen of all Mini Mk II models.

was combined with a lighter diaphragm spring clutch for most models. At the end of 1964 the engineers modified the gearbox output shaft yet again with a further improved oil-seal.

By this time all Minis had key starting, necessitating the introduction of a solenoid into the starter circuit.

Sporting experience had shown that the highly stressed engine oil had to be checked frequently, to avoid thickening or even the formation of sludge. All drivers of 1965 Minis had a warning light on the dash which indicated a blocked oil filter and the need to change oil and filter. All these changes meant that the 1965 models cost some 4% more than previously.

A great event happened in the autumn of the same year: Mini drivers could say goodbye to gearchanging, for the world's smallest automatic gearbox, specially developed by Automotive Products, was announced. All constituent parts were housed in the engine sump and, uniquely, were lubricated by the circulating engine oil. This announcement at the end of 1965 was perhaps premature, and because of many problems the Mini Automatic only became

available in quantity from 1967. Early testing revealed that oil surge in the sump under cornering could cause oil starvation of the torque converter and sky-high engine revs. To compensate for this rather basic failing the oil pump was moved to the centre of the sump, and sump capacity was increased as well.

Final assembly problems also arose, and manufacture of the gearboxes was transferred to clinically clean, dust free rooms to ensure a dependable assembly of the unit with its numerous hydraulic valves.

The design itself put all known hydraulic 'boxes in the shade and, to make the most of the engine's meagre output, gave four forward speeds as against the three or even two of other automatic transmissions current at the time. The two-speed Powerglide transmission fitted to the Vauxhall Victor 101, for instance, made an already underpowered car sluggish in the extreme, and did nothing for the reputation of automatic transmissions when applied to the wrong vehicles. Apart from the automatic function, a floor-mounted central lever in a chromed quadrant enabled manual overriding at any time. The quadrant indicator showed not only neutral, automatic

The Countryman was promoted as the ideal family and leisure vehicle. The sliding rear windows were a practical feature.

and reverse, but also markings for the four speeds.

A mechanical control ensured gear selection according to load when in automatic mode, and there was also a kick-down working directly from the throttle pedal.

To compensate for the usual power loss, the compression ratio was increased to 9:1 and a larger SU carburettor with modified inlet manifold was fitted. Power rose to 39.5bhp at 5250rpm and torque of 44lb/ft peaked at 2500rpm instead of 2900 – a respectable figure for a single-carburettor 850cc engine.

The same recipe was used for the automatic-transmission version of the Mini 1000 in 1967 to compensate for power lost through the torque converter. The 998cc engine, producing 38.5bhp, had an 8.9:1 compression ratio and the revised manifold with HS-4 carburettor. Power went up to 41.5bhp, torque remaining the same at 52lb/ft but at a lower 2400rpm. Gear changes on a briskly driven Mini 1000 took place at 28mph, 42mph and 55mph. Driven more gently, upward changes came at 11, 16 and 21mph, thus the engine was working at comparatively low revs.

The Mini has continued to undergo detail and major

Mini unit with automatic transmission in the sump, running in the engine oil. To keep the oil clean a larger oil filter (next to the starter) was used.

changes throughout its life. In 1966, for example, the Elf and Hornet Mk III appeared, with concealed door hinges and wind-up windows – changes that were to appear throughout the Mini range in due course.

After the introduction of the Mark III doors, interior equipment was re-worked to include fresh air inlets on the parcel shelf of the Hornet and on the dash of the Elf. In October 1967, two years before production ended, there were new seats and steering column stalks for lights, indicators and headlamp flasher. Automatic transmission was finally available and manual cars received an all-synchromesh gearbox in August 1968.

Wolseley and Riley automatics are exceedingly rare due to a production run of barely two years – production of the big-booted variants stopped quietly in August 1969. Only 28,455 Hornets were constructed and the Elf was not notably more successful – 30,912 saw the light of day – but that makes the Wolseley and Riley desirable today.

However they were not notably successful in the new car market in their day. BMC's subsidiary company in South Africa used the Elf/Hornet bodyshell design in conjunction with the much simpler nose of the normal Mini. This version became known, at least locally, as the 'Mini Mk III'.

The first automatic-transmission prototype was running in 1962. The kickdown cable from carburettor to gearbox can be seen.

South African 'Mini Mk III' – Elf/Hornet bodyshell with normal Mini nose.

Many MINI Inspirations

Issigonis' front-wheel-drive concept inspired alternatives and variants from the very beginning; some progressed but were abandoned, some took shape. Even during the project stage of the Mini there was a rear-engined design at Longbridge: it arose from a collaboration with Laurence Pomeroy from *The Motor* and was intended to have a transverse in-line four-cylinder at the rear. From today's viewpoint this vehicle might have been the basis for the German NSU Prinz – but Austin did not take the project very far. At Morris at Cowley Charles Griffin, an ex-Wolseley man, planned another rear-engined vehicle known as DO19. He was certain that he could provide even more room than Issigonis on the same basic surface. The mock-up had sliding doors and it did provide more room than the Mini, for above the rear-mounted twin-cylinder engine there was some luggage space. On the other hand, the legs of the front seat occupants were ahead of the front axle line (as in the VW Kombi and the

The potentially dangerous seating position for driver and front-seat passenger can be clearly seen in this mock up of DO19.

Longbridge built this four-door prototype as early as 1960. It had concealed door hinges but all four doors had sliding windows.

Fiat Multipla) and thus very exposed even in minor frontal impact collisions. This was reason enough for the project to be abandoned.

Around 1960 a four-door Mini project was developed on a longer wheelbase. This was promising, but it did not reach production because of stability and cost factors. Also, the four-door vehicle would have been considerably heavier than the production two-door, resulting in a loss of performance. Yet this four-door prototype is important for it shows that the solution to problems with the concealed door hinges had been found as early as the beginning of the 1960s. The whereabouts of this four-door is not known; a second vehicle was built privately for the London-Mexico rally in 1970. It retired on an early rally 'prime' in Yugoslavia and never got to South America. After having been out of the limelight for more than twenty years, this car surfaced again in England in early 1992.

In the 1960s Austin's long-serving designer Dick Burzi looked into a variety of Mini themes. He created the different front and rear ends for the Elf and Hornet. His favourite though was a little beach car with wickerwork seats, which was built in different designs but small numbers. Basically these beach cars had no doors, but retained the fixed roof of the production car. Issigonis loved them more than his Moke; one result was that big hotels in the Caribbean and Hawaii were able to buy Mini and Riley beach cars. For the Riley, Burzi took the front end of the Australian Mini and combined it with a new honeycomb grille, adding more chrome than some thought good for it.

Simultaneously, BMC looked at modified versions for specific markets and the green light was given for an Australian model. Introduced in 1961, this was badged as a Morris, always had wind-up windows, a mechanical fuel pump for the 998cc engine and windscreen wipers that parked automatically. The Australian Mini 850 always had the rubber suspension – the Hydrolastic kind was reserved for the more expensive de Luxe with the Hornet engine. In 1969 a version known as the Mini K was launched from the Sydney plant.

In Denmark the Mini could not be called Mini, because the name had been registered for a town car that was never built, so the Austin Seven became the 'Austin Partner' and the Morris Mini-Minor the 'Morris Mascot'.

BMC was ambitious to expand into developing countries and made every effort to set up local production. For Chile, this meant creating the Mini anew but in plastic, for there was no steel industry in South America. Longbridge created prototypes without guttering; flanged wheel arches were replaced by pronounced bulges and, in a number of places, load-bearing parts became almost 10mm thick. Because of the uncertain political situation, the Chilean licence manufacture came to nothing –

This beach car for hotels had a new nose as well as the more obvious open sides and wicker seats.

Gianni and Elio Zagato built this sports coupé using Mini subframes – the bodywork appeared very advanced but was much too heavy.

Cars for Denmark had this badge.

The plastic prototype for Chile; it is recognizable by the missing rain gutters and stiffening flanges.

The 15th anniversary was marked at the end of the production line. This awkward bumper was found on later cars for Canada.

Minor changes enabled Nuccio Bertone to provide the Mini-Cooper with an up-market appearance.

In Pininfarina's 9X much of the Mini's 'personality' was lost.

The beginnings of the Mini Clubman can be seen in this Roy Haynes design.

This vehicle was destined for the 1967 World Fair in Montreal; during a record attempt 24 ladies were crammed into it.

Ernest Marples' one-off hatchback Mini-Cooper.

although some 10 cars were built. The experimental cars are preserved by the British Motor Industry Heritage Trust. A later project for production in Israel, including the plastic-bodied Mini developed by Jem Marsh, is referred to in the chapter on Mini specials.

A singularly ugly variation was produced for export to Canada in the 1970s, because that market required bumpers 6½in higher than normal and reflectors on the sides of front and rear wings. This model also had a more powerful heater and de-toxed exhaust. It was made on the normal production line.

In 1966 John Cooper sent a complete Mini Cooper to Bertone in Italy, as he sought to compete in the increasing market for exclusive Minis. Externally the car had an attractive grille with a fine honeycomb, rectangular flashers in front and quarter lights in the front doors, which also provided front channels for the wind-up windows. In front of the rear wheels, the insignia of Carrozzeria Bertone discreetly showed the world that this was a specially equipped Mini. Leather-covered bucket

seats front and back with integral head rests, electric window lifts, and instruments fitted into a polished aluminium dash underlined the special equipment. Series production did not follow and John Cooper ultimately preferred to collaborate closely with Radford, Crayford and others.

BMC had a great liking for stunts to demonstrate to the public the Mini's image. For the World Fair in Montreal they painted a Mini overall with a Union Jack for a record attempt: how many young ladies would fit into a Mini – answer: 24!

The then British Minister of Transport, Ernest Marples, took delivery of a Cooper S with a hatch-back and a folding back seat – this concept unfortunately never went into production.

For years BMC could not refrain from searching for a suitable successor to the immortal Mini – fortunately without success. The most harmonious attempt was the 9X, which had more elbow room due to its convex sides, but avoided 'fashionable' influences. In fact the 9X was the precursor for cars such as Fiesta and Polo; it could almost hold its own as a new creation even today. The engine from the 9X was used in Issigonis' gearless Mini project of 1975.

Stylist Roy Haynes toyed with other detail modifications. Apart from the changed Clubman nose, he proposed to give the Mini a built-out tail with an enlarged boot.

For other design jobs Italian studios were favoured. Pininfarina was responsible for sporting derivatives in the 1960s, notably ADO34. Built on a Minivan wheelbase, with engine and running gear from a 1275 Cooper S, this was an open two-seater seen as a possible MG Midget replacement. ADO35, also by Pininfarina, was a parallel coupé project. In 1970 the ADO70 Targa-roof 2+2 was designed at Longbridge on the basis of a 1275GT. One was built by Michelotti, emerging as a heavy-weight car with sluggish performance. Its lines also dated more than the earlier Pininfarina essay, and it would not have stood up too well against the competition of the Fiat X1/9 that came a little later (at around the time that ADO70 could have reached the production stage). An intention had been to produce it for the US market, but there was some concern that it would not meet safety regulations. These stylish

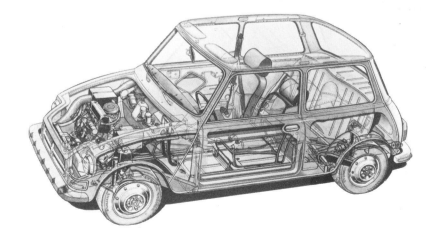

This BMC experimental vehicle was a Mini modified to demonstrate a crumple zone and passive safety devices. It ran on Denovo safety wheels and the low nose was intended to give pedestrians some protection.

The Maximini is an optical illusion – the joins in this super-wide joke car are visible.

projects suffered the same fate as Dick Burzi's Austin-Healey/MG sports car essays, but at least ADO34 and ADO70 survive, in running order, in the British Motor Industry Heritage Trust museum.

The ultra-wide Mini was a 1973 publicity exercise. The rally-Maximini of 1967 was, of course, a press stunt. Many still believe today that the vehicle actually existed. The truth was that two Minis were placed side by side, separated by one car's width. A cleverly made sheet metal centre piece joined the two cars, which at a glance appeared to be one vehicle. This metal cover formed the roof, bonnet centre, widened grille and the straight centre section of the bumper. The whole was carefully placed on the centre line of the two parked Minis. Windscreens were painted matt from within and the screen area of the metal cover was also painted. To conceal the two inner front wheels of the basic Minis, a metal apron like those protecting the oil sump extended to the ground....

Super minis from the top houses

Britain has always had many coachbuilders making high-class bodies for Rolls-Royce, Bentley, Daimler and other leading marques. No-one would have believed that the Mini would one day be a basis for their craftsmanship. The actor Peter Sellers decided that he wanted a very special Mini with basketwork side panels. The Hooper coachworks undertook the job and showed the car at the 1963 London Motor Show. The black car with its red roof and yellow sides encouraged Corgi to make a model of it.

Quickly, other specialists followed the new trend: Crayford specialized in cabriolets, while Harold Radford preferred estate cars. Suddenly there were a lot of up-market Minis available, much favoured by TV and film personalities and potentates of the Gulf states for driving round London. Britt Ekland had a Mini with a hatchback, built by Harold Radford. While that solution was not as elegant as the Transport Minister's 'Shopper', promotion by such well known people filled the order books of the Mini improvers

Basket work recalling private carriages of the past; the late Peter Sellers considered this as chic for his Mini.

and re-builders. When Radford's marketing man Eddie Collins moved over to Wood & Pickett, their business flourished and their specials, called 'Margrave', were produced in some numbers, despite very high prices. Some of the Mini conversion specialists are recalled here, and although most have ceased trading their efforts have firm places in Mini history.

Automobilia

Specialists in accessories and components, this company followed the Wood & Pickett example and called their Mini

luxury variants Phaeton. These had vinyl roofs, opera windows, tinted glass and other gimmicks, but at around half the price of a Wood & Pickett car. They accepted used Minis as the basis for their rebuilds.

Broadspeed

Older racing people recall Ralph Broad as having been responsible for superbly tuned engines. On the Mini side,

Automobilia's Phaeton was similar to Wood & Pickett's creation, at only half the price.

The Broadspeed GT.

▼ Crayford Convertible Saloon, with rear side windows retained.

Broadspeed produced a fastback coupé, with its rear somewhat in the style of the Aston Martin DB5, generally painted in two colours and with Minilite alloy wheels. Its basis was the Cooper S; the track was widened and the seam running down the front wings was eliminated. It was 2in/5cm lower than the original, so the screen was raked, and the new tail extended the overall length by 10in/25cm. Some 28 of these Broadspeed GTs left the workshops in Birmingham before the company turned to other tasks.

Crayford

Crayford made its reputation with a Mini convertible, leaving window frames in situ and with a soft top folding right back onto the rear shelf. This required considerable body stiffening – reinforcement from the A posts to B, stiffening ribs between the latter below the rear seating,

The Crayford full convertible differed from the convertible-saloon in not having rear side windows.

▼ Crayford's Mini Moke in 'Surrey' form.

extended reinforcements of the B posts and extra metal above the bootlid aperture. The car shown in 1963 unfortunately sported ugly auxiliary lights in a housing on the bonnet, something like the taxi signs on black taxi roofs—it soon came to be known as 'nose for hire'. Nevertheless its commercial success was considerable – the modifications cost some £150 at the time. These 1966 Crayford Convertibles made their impact in the British press because the Heinz company offered 57 Wolseley Hornet convertibles as prizes in a jubilee competition. On

these models the rear side windows remained in place. Crayford converted some 800 Minis into the two types of fun-mobiles. For a time the firm in Westerham also worked over the unloved Moke to remove its paramilitary aura. Called 'Surrey-Moke', some 20 vehicles were made for foreign customers. A white one with red and white striped top was used in the television serial 'The Prisoner'.

ERA Mini Turbo

Engineering Research and Application Ltd has its origin in the one-time racing car constructor ERA, and when the last ERA racing project was sold to Bristol Cars in 1953 the firm concentrated on work for Zenith, later Solex. In 1986 it was acquired by the Jack Knight Group and, while continuing consultancy work, looked to building cars again. The ERA Mini Turbo was a step towards that goal. It was announced in 1989 as a car that would have all the characteristics of the Mini Cooper S. To a degree that was overtaken as Rover re-introduced the Mini Cooper, but in fact there was a place for the Mini Turbo in a higher performance class – this was the fastest Mini to be built in numbers (and the quantities were not small, as late in 1990 ERA delivered its first batch of 247 cars to Japan). Incidentally, this turbo car came some 28 years after Allard had tried a supercharged Mini.

The familiar 1275 A series engine was used, turbocharged to give 96bhp at 6130 rpm, with good torque and mid-

Denis Adams' work gave the ERA Mini Turbo chunky lines, accentuated by cast wheels with the three interlinked circles of the ERA badge.

range performance. Somehow space was found in the engine compartment for a Garrett T3 turbocharger, and the water and oil cooling systems had to be modified. The front suspension was revised, particularly to minimize torque steer. While ventilated disc brakes were fitted at the front, drums were retained at the rear.

The visible body modifications and spoilers were the work of Denis Adams, the Marcos designer. But the biggest non-mechanical changes were inside the car, where supportive 'sports-style' seats were used and the steering column changed to do away with the old 'bus driver' position.

Claimed top speed for the Mini Turbo was 110mph/177kmh, with 0-60mph acceleration in 7.8 sec. It could hold its own in the sporting hatchback class, and it showed that there is indeed life in the 30-year-old Mini.

Compared to the production Mini, the Sprint with its shallower side windows and modified sides appeared flattened.

Minisprint

Mini enthusiasts get that look in their eyes when the 'Sprint' is mentioned. The name stood for competent chopping and customizing – as far as the Mini was concerned that meant lowering it as much as possible without too much change in its appearance and matching these looks with improved performance. The idea came from racing driver Neville Trickett around 1966. To achieve this looks easy today but was much more difficult then. Trickett not only cut off the roof but had to change the bodywork below the window line, which meant altering the bulkhead and even the inner wings. New bonnets and boot lids were needed, and the external body was discarded. The first Minisprints were built by Sigma and were 3in/7.5cm lower than the standard car; later examples were 4in/10cm lower. Smaller round Cibié headlights had to give way to rectangular units to meet legal requirements.

All this work resulted in a high price; a Minisprint never cost less than three times the price of a Mini, but one bought intoxicating performance and road-holding. After less than a year the BMC main dealers Stewart & Arden obtained all rights to the Minisprint, but did not develop the car and it went quietly to its rest at the end of 1967. Some of the much loved Sprints are fortunately in the hands of British enthusiasts.

Radford

Harold Radford's main operation was rebuilding production vehicles into utilities or shooting brakes, as they were called. The company also made hearses and ambulances, and even converted Rolls-Royce, Aston Martin and Jaguar models into estate cars. When Mini mania became the fashion, Peter Sellers went to Radfords and made the firm into his own car couturier. After the basket-work Mini, his wife Britt Ekland also wanted a motorized shopping trolley; this she obtained in 1965 in the shape of a Mini de Ville GT with a hatchback – and suddenly a lot of other ladies required a Mini with a large hatch. As early as 1963 Radford exhibited a Cooper de Ville Grand Luxe, a black and silver vehicle with sun roof, leather upholstery and every possible gadget. But in 1966 Radford's marketing chief went to Wood & Pickett, taking a large number of

customers with him. In spite of this, the 1963 prototype was re-built into a 1275S and advertised for £1650. Some modifications were also incorporated in the design of the hatchback, and production reached full capacity of three cars a week. The company was sold at the end of the 1960s and Harold Radford died in the late 1980s.

Late in 1990 the Mini de Ville was revived by Harold Radford (Coachbuilding) Ltd and the first of a batch was completed – most were destined for Japan, where any sort of Mini is a cult car. True to the original the Radford Mini of the 1990s was a luxury vehicle, with leather and walnut very evident inside, fittings such as electric windows, and almost incidentally a 1275 engine.

Britt Ekland's Radford Mini hatchback.

Trevor James

The success of the gentrified Wood & Pickett Mini inspired not only Automobilia but also Trevor James Car Conversions in St Albans to modify the Mini, with cheaper ways to a similar end product. James began with the

Trevor James used Vauxhall lights for the long-nosed Mini.

31

For Prince Tenenggong of Brunei only the best was good enough. He ordered special tuning from racing driver John Sprinzel and Wood & Pickett customized the car. The modifications to this flower-power Mini cost £4000.

Clubman, which received strange bumpers, new plastic grilles and the usual internal equipment. James made sure that the conversions were offered at half the price demanded by W&P; experts claimed this showed in the use of poorer materials and superficial workmanship. Despite this, the company succeeded with its upmarket Mini for some ten years.

Wood & Pickett

Apart from modifying the normal Mini, Wood & Pickett also reworked the Elf, Hornet and Clubman, all with the usual extensive equipment and external modifications. Until the oil crisis at the beginning of the 1970s, the Mini business was only a sideline, for modifying luxury limousines was much more rewarding. The Mini conversions benefitted from the many cars that passed through their workshops. Jaguar switchgear, lights from Vauxhall and Cibié, and comfortable seats were incorporated in luxurious Minis which sometimes had cocktail bars, TV, air conditioning, tinted windows, electric window lifts as well as wooden facias, door cappings, etc. One of the prettiest was a Mini with Mercedes headlamps and black tinted glass, and the car with the most chic had

no rear side windows, only a little oval rear screen and hood irons. The sumptuous interior had hand-sewn leather sports seats (in colours to order). Including special tuning and chassis changes, prices were up to £20,000, and a used example at a favourable price is well worth having.

———

The many other Mini modifiers or those who offered parts and conversion sets would over-extend this chapter. But there was Brian Luff who offered 'Rolls-Royce' grilles, until the gentlemen in Crewe stopped him; then there was the Redbird-GFK front grille, very similar to the Ridgway Conversion at only £24, and a one piece plastic bonnet called Cuda from the Coventry based Woodway Studios for only £21. Mini enthusiasm attracted many a small manufacturer; if all else fails, enthusiasts do the job themselves.

▶ Cabriolet by L&H of Frankfurt, with flared wheel arches and paintwork in British Racing Green.

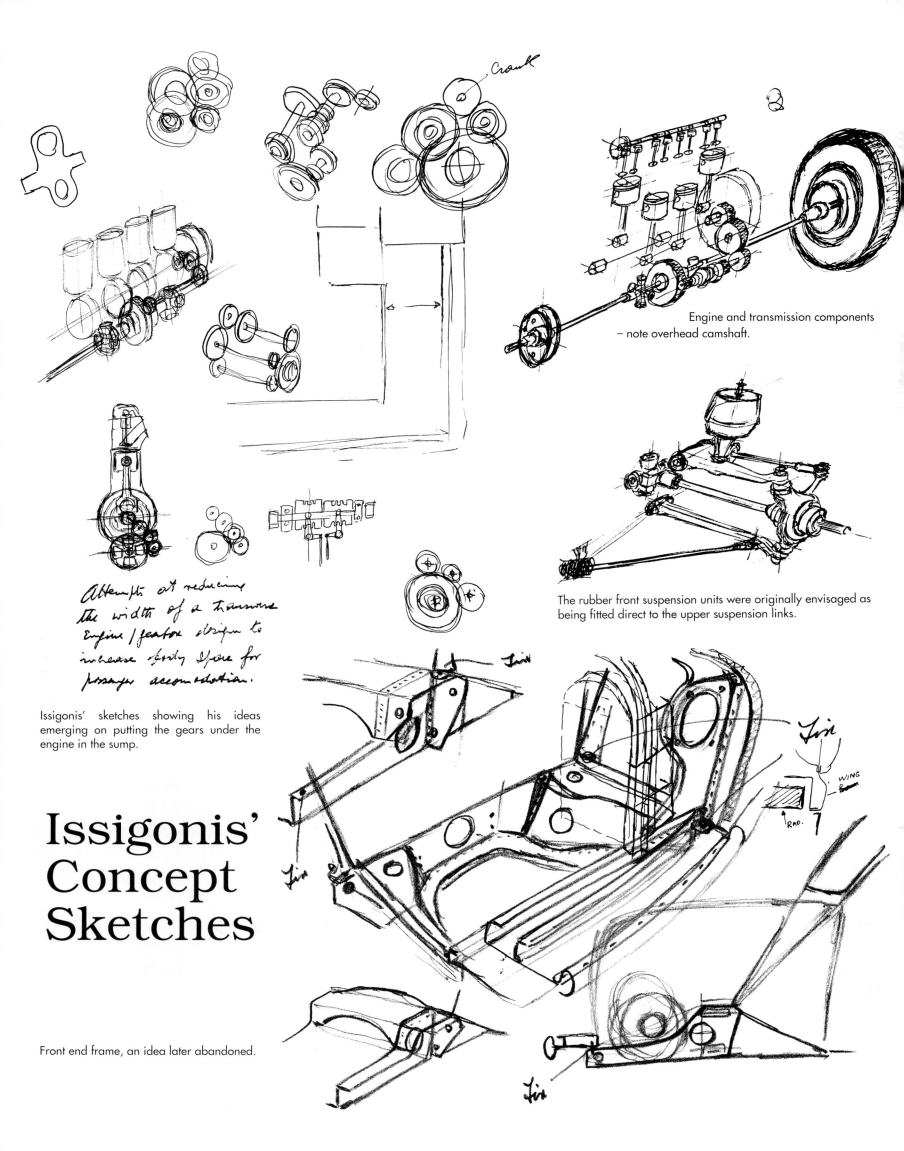

Crank

Engine and transmission components
– note overhead camshaft.

The rubber front suspension units were originally envisaged as
being fitted direct to the upper suspension links.

*Attempts at reducing
the width of a transverse
Engine/gearbox design to
increase body space for
passenger accomodation.*

Issigonis' sketches showing his ideas
emerging on putting the gears under the
engine in the sump.

Issigonis'
Concept
Sketches

Front end frame, an idea later abandoned.

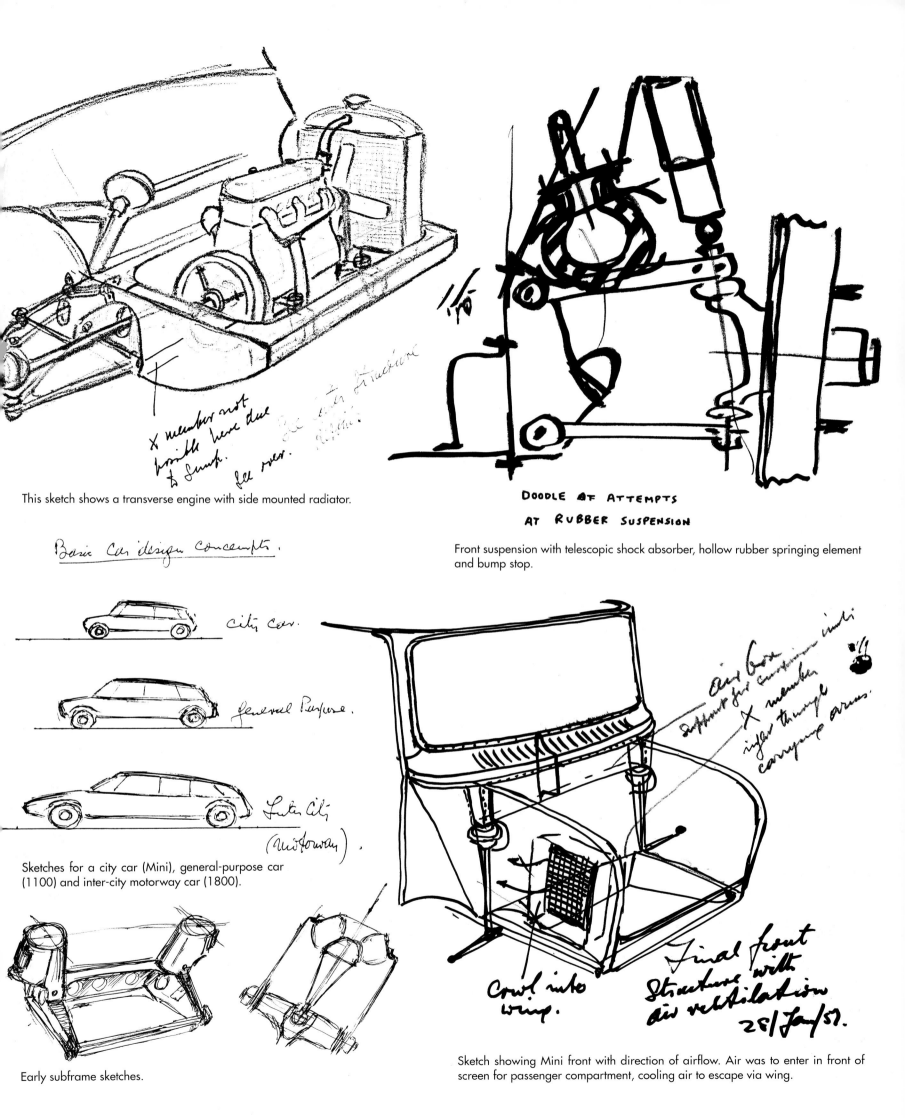

This sketch shows a transverse engine with side mounted radiator.

Basic Car design Concepts.

Sketches for a city car (Mini), general-purpose car (1100) and inter-city motorway car (1800).

Early subframe sketches.

DOODLE OF ATTEMPTS AT RUBBER SUSPENSION

Front suspension with telescopic shock absorber, hollow rubber springing element and bump stop.

Sketch showing Mini front with direction of airflow. Air was to enter in front of screen for passenger compartment, cooling air to escape via wing.

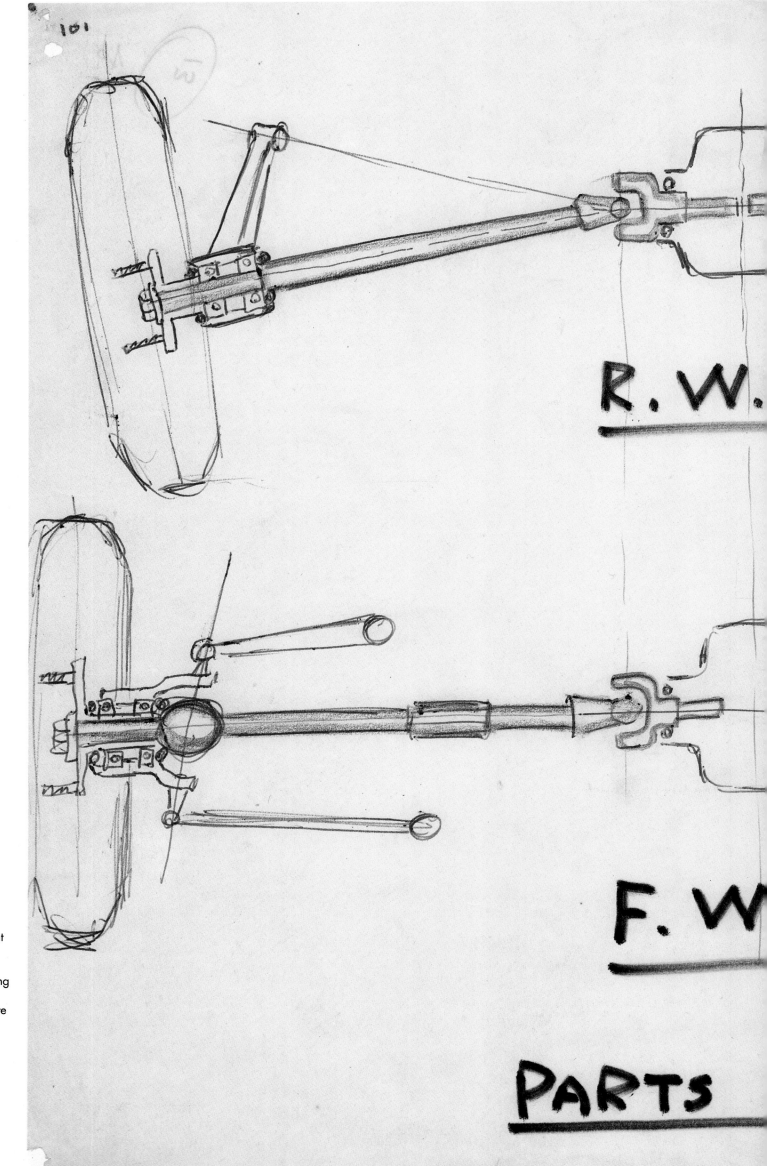

R. W.

F. W.

PARTS

Comparison of front and rear wheel drive. Issigonis contemplated sliding joints for the drive shafts to compensate for suspension movements.

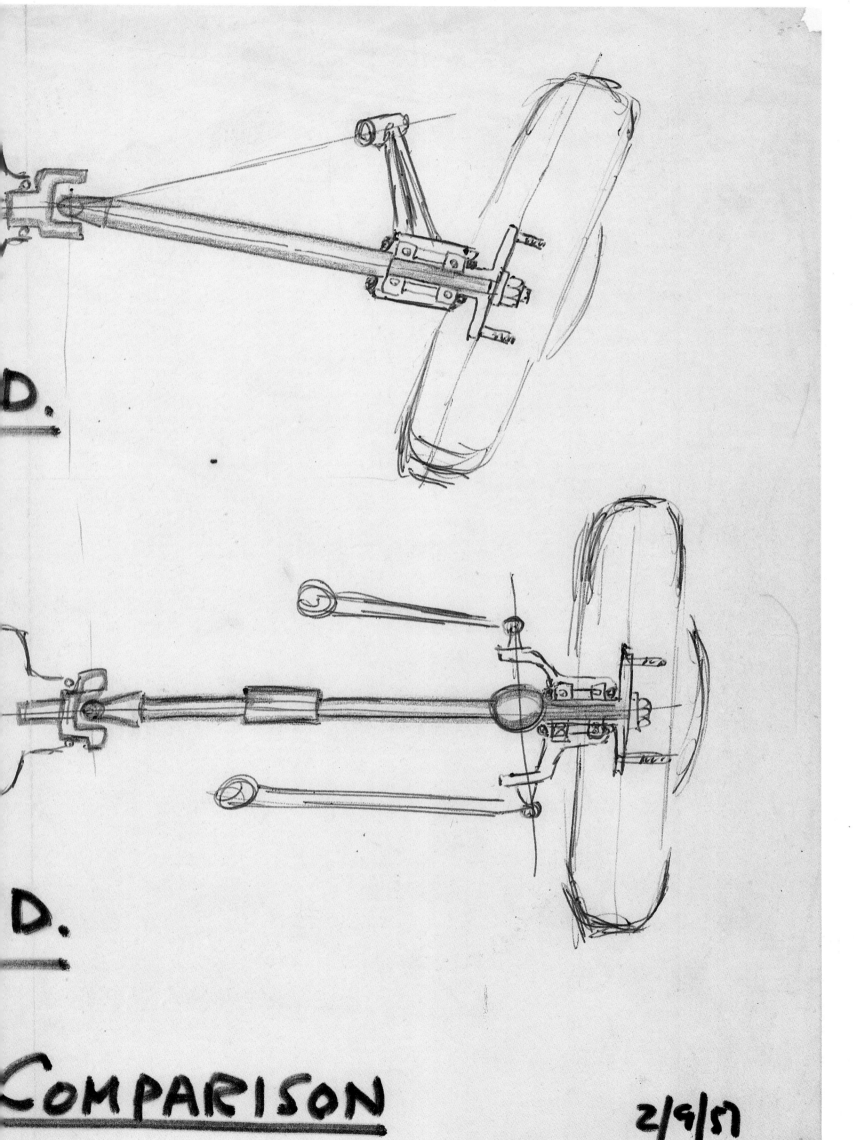

D.

D.

COMPARISON

2/9/57

MINI Acquires a Family

The specification of ADO15 (Austin Drawing Office 15) was finalized on 26th August 1959 when the Austin Seven and Morris Mini-Minor were announced. Chassis number A/A2S7/101 began the Austin's family history and the first Morris was M/A2S4/101. The maker is shown before the oblique, the A was for engine size, 2S for two-door saloon body and the 7 or 4 was for the series of model within the Austin or Morris genealogy. The standard and de Luxe models were introduced simultaneously and differed only in the wheel trims and interior trim. The Austin grille had wavy horizontal chrome strips, the Morris grille was simpler and resembled the version fitted to the Minivan and Pickup. In September 1960 the Traveller with side windows was announced; its rear was fitted with woodwork in the style of the popular Morris Minor Traveller and it was sold from the showrooms as the Austin 'Countryman' or Morris 'Mini-Traveller'. Both of these were 130in/330cm long, 10in/25cm more than the basic car, and had a 4in/10cm longer wheelbase. Dry weight went up, of course, but the new models could take some 110lbs/50kg more load.

From May 1961, and beginning with chassis number A/A2S7/123291 for Austin and M/A2S4/70376 for Morris, strengthened suspension cones were introduced.

September 1961 saw the addition of the Super saloon to the range; it had an oval instrument panel with oil pressure and water temperature gauges, lever-type door handles, better trim, key starting and two-tone paint.

The 'Seven' name – and the appalling 'Se7en' rendering – were dropped at the beginning of 1962 and 'Mini' became the type designation for the Austins although the Morris version was badged Mini-Minor until 1969. As the public could not really distinguish between the de Luxe and Super saloon, the advantages of both models were combined in the Super de Luxe in October 1962. Apart from this, synchromesh on the top three gears was improved in series production. Considerable demand from tradesmen, business people and public services and authorities resulted in the introduction of a new version of the estate car without the woodwork, slightly cheaper and often preferred in export markets.

The first really major change came in 1964 with the introduction of the new Hydrolastic interconnected suspension, only available on the saloons and destined to continue in production until 1971.The brakes were also improved, the shoes having two anchorage points. From November the driver's seat had a three-position adjustment.

The year 1965 saw the introduction of the automatic gearbox – for a car of that size a complete novelty at the time, apart from various forms of clutch assistance like the Standrive or the belt-drive system of the DAF. Power losses through the transmission were compensated for by

Minivans had a painted grille and a minimum of equipment.

Riley Elf Mk II still did not have wind-up windows. It also featured Hydrolastic suspension (from 1964) and the 998cc engine giving 40bhp at 5250rpm.

Publicity photograph of the launch of the Austin Seven in 1959.

One of the first Austin Minis.

Early Mini production at Longbridge.

Issigonis at Longbridge with the first production Mini-Minor and a 1965 model.

Interior of the automatic Mini, showing the slender gear selector lever in its quadrant.

fitting a bigger carburettor and other detail modifications; engine power rose a little.

The door handles fitted to the Super de Luxe in place of the inner pull-cord had an unfortunate taste for catching in men's jacket pockets – complaints multiplied and in January 1966 a protective shield was at last fitted.

The first major facelift came with the introduction of the Mk II in October 1967. There was a new grille shape with more squared-off corners and a wide chrome surround replacing the earlier eyebrow. The march of rationalization meant that Austin and Morris models now differed only in badging and grille pattern, Austins having plain horizontal bars, Morris models horizontal and vertical bars. Improvements included revised interiors with new seats, but the exterior door-hinges and sliding windows were kept. At the rear the Mk II could be recognized by the larger rear lamps and wider rear screen. The majority of these changes were also incorporated in the Cooper and Cooper S. On non-Cooper Austin and Morris Mk II models the 998cc engine was available for the first time.

In July 1968 all models got inner door handles instead of the pull-cords, rally experience brought plastic fan blades into series production and from September 1968 a new engine number series starting from 101 indicated the use of an all-synchromesh gearbox.

Two years after the arrival of the Mk II, another major innovation took place: some nine years after its first production, a new edition of the Mini came out, code-named ADO20. Now Mini drivers could wind their windows down and the doors had lost their outside hinges – an expensive re-design. No-one seems to know what prompted the elimination of the Hydrolastic suspension from the 850 and 1000 Mini, but they were now fitted with the old rubber cone suspension, and this reversion applied to the Clubman and GT models in 1971. To satisfy export markets and the trend to international standardization, the fathers of ADO20 at last gave up the positive earth system in favour of the negative earth, soon combined with an alternator.

From April 1969 the makers supplied the 850 Mini on demand with a heated rear window, but only at the end of October was interference-free ignition fitted.

The pick-up, spartan, durable, practical and, like all Minis, great fun to drive.

The next years brought many detail modifications and, from time to time, some special series. The gearshift on all models gave way to a slicker remote control shift in 1973, while door hanging, carburation, ignition and many other aspects were improved. Mini 850 standard equipment was improved by adding a passenger sun visor, inertia reel seatbelts and rear window demisting, also radial tyres from May 1976. These, together with a redesigned front subframe, with six rubber mountings and retuned suspension rates, brought about better roadholding. From August 1977 the Mini received a new steering wheel, and matt-black painted bumpers and larger pedals followed in August 1978.

Prior to the works holidays in July 1979 a new basic 850 series was introduced. This Mini City was a simpler version – all chromed parts including the guttering were now in matt black. The body sides sported triple stripes and a City logo and seats wore a black and white checked cloth.

Simultaneously British Leyland offered a Super de Luxe version of the 850 to mark the end of production of the smallest-capacity model in the range. Apart from extra instruments and cloth-covered seats, purchasers got face-level air vents on the dash, opening windows at the rear, map pockets on the seatbacks and in the doors, matt-black wheel arch trims and a coachline under the window line.

In 1967 a bigger-engined Mini had been introduced, in the form of the 1000, a 998cc-engined saloon and estate. For the next two years the Austin and Morris models co-existed, only differentiated by badging. Both had the new grille shape but with different grille patterns, chrome wheel trims and all the Mk II equipment. The sliding windows and outside hinges were still present and the cord pulls for the

This publicity photo demonstrates the practical value of the door bins in sliding-window Minis. Note the position of the chassis plates, suggesting that this car is an export mode).

doors only disappeared in July 1968.

The Mini 1000 in Mk II form was built for a mere two years, so this model is a rare species even today. In October 1969,

Morris Mini Mk II, launched in October 1967 along with the Mk II Austin Mini. The Austin grille had horizontal bars only.

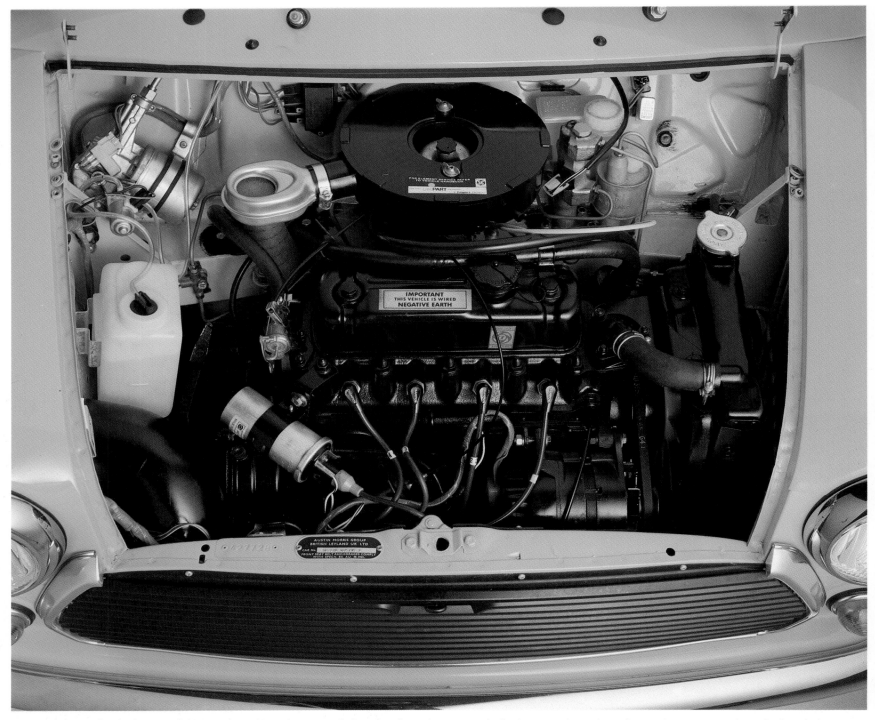

Accessibility under the bonnet of the Mini has always been good, though a few jobs – particularly changing the radiator bottom hose – are awkward. The whole engine/drive unit comes out in one piece on its subframe, the body being raised to allow it to come out underneath.

as described earlier, British Leyland revised the whole model range and the resulting ADO20 represented a considerable improvement. Even non-experts noted the hidden door hinges and the wind-up windows. In Australia the 1.1 litre Mini K on similar lines was launched (some 176,000 Minis were built in Australia).

The efforts of chief stylist Roy Haynes to modernize the Mini took shape as the Clubman, a long-nosed variant which appeared in the showrooms, like the ADO20 models, in 1969. According to Haynes' ideas the Clubman was to have had a longer rear with a lid à la Hillman Imp, but he did not get approval for this idea due to the existence of the Riley Elf and Wolseley Hornet. Using the styling buck of the ADO20, he added – apart from the enlarged nose and tail – new

◀ The Mk II range, including Elf, Hornet and the 'woody' Traveller. The last series of Minivan and Pickup only had the old painted grilles.

bumpers and front quarterlights, the latter because he was afraid that there would not be room in the door for the window lifting gear due to having to 'hide' the door-hinges. Thanks to the convex door skins it became possible to move the window lifts so far to the outside that the quarter lights could be dispensed with (but the Italian Innocenti Mini kept them).

The Clubman looked at the world with a grille extending over the car's full width; in its first form it had three double strips of chrome between the round headlamps, with a vertical Mini Clubman badge. Side lamps and flashers were fitted below the bumper, separated from the number plate mounting by vertical overriders. Dimensions for the new Clubman changed: length was increased to 125in/ 317cm (estate car, 134in/340cm) and unladen weight of the saloon rose to 1406lb/638kg, making it the heaviest Mini yet.

With the launch of the Clubman the regular Mini estate

The Austin Mini Mk II 1000 de Luxe with 998cc and 38bhp. The Austin badge is now round, the bumpers have new overriders and there are new door handles.

ADO20 ('Mk III') 1000 showing the enlarged rear screen, wind-up windows and concealed door hinges.

The City 850 cost £2280 on its introduction in August 1979. Exterior trim was matt black, there were chequered seats and side stripes – only the miniskirt was out of fashion. It ran for only a year.

A late Mini 850 on the move.

Interior of the City 850 with cloth seat panels: rather a far cry from the interior of the early Mini.

For the Mini's 20th Anniversary there was another special model. The planned run of 2500 silver-grey or pink-metallic cars soon became 5000. This 1100 Special was much in demand due to its £3300 price.

The interior of the 1100 Special sported smart cloth-covered seats, a central console with radio and clock and a special steering wheel (from the Innocenti 90/120).

The Clubman Estate originally boasted a double chrome strip on its side, with imitation wood fillet. There was a BL badge behind the front wheel and twin wing mirrors were standard.

The Sprite LE had a production run of 2500. It was equipped with light-alloy wheels, stripes and wheel arch extensions.

Morris-badged left hand drive Mk II.

The Clubman, first introduced in 1969, got a mixed reception.

The Clubman 1275GT, badged Mini 1275GT, had a wider track, rally stripes and Rostyle wheels.

was phased out. No-one realized then that the days of the Cooper S were also numbered, for the luxurious 1275GT was waiting in the wings. Whilst it had 60bhp against the Cooper's 77, it only took 3 seconds more to the magic 60mph and could manage an acceptable 87mph. It was well equipped and had the servo-assisted discs from the Cooper S, which was to be built until June 1971.

Inside the Clubman, the buyer had the feeling of sitting in a different car; the characteristic central instrument had given place to a rectangular binnacle above the steering column, which housed the round speedometer (with mileometer) on the left and a combined fuel gauge and water temperature gauge on the right. Below the three-spoke steering wheel on the right was a combined stalk for the flashers and horn – only in 1977 was another stalk fitted on the left to operate wipers and windscreen washers. The parcel shelf held a panel fitted with rocker switches for lights and hazard flashers and the two usual Mini push/pull controls. The left one worked the choke by pulling it out and twisting to fix it. The right hand one continued to confuse all non-Mini drivers: pulled out fully and almost touching the knee it switched off the heating; pushed in, warm air circulated through the heater matrix and a distributor lever under the dash directed warm air either up or down. The top edge of the dash was padded and face-level air vents were fitted at each end of the parcel shelf.

The following years brought few changes to the Clubman

and the 1000. The Hydrolastic suspension was once again deleted from all models in 1971 – probably for economy reasons. It had happened to the 850 and 1000 Mini in 1969 when ADO20 was introduced. All engine and transmission changes to the 850 were incorporated into the Mini 1000 and Clubman.

In October 1975 the first 'limited edition' Mini, the 1000 Special, appeared on the UK market, recognizable by its coachline, external mirrors and colour – it was only available in dark Brooklands Green and Glacier White. There were reclining seats with orange striped covers and sand-coloured carpets.

This 1000 Special had the HS-4 carburettor on a revised inlet manifold, a new air filter and revised ignition settings, bringing output to 40bhp. The automatic version had a slightly raised compression ratio at 8:9:1 and put out 41.5bhp at 4850rpm. Maximum torque remained the same for both versions at 52lb/ft at 2700rpm.

In 1975 the Clubman engine was enlarged by 100cc, delivering 45bhp at 5250rpm, but automatics kept the original engine size.

In May 1976 came a rear screen demister, radial tyres, new mountings for the subframes, moulded carpets and enlarged pedals. Externally there was a new grille and different badges.

The Mini HLE was available from April 1982, recognizable by new wheel trims and matt black grille.

In August 1977 more goodies were added to the Clubman: tinted glass and reversing lights, locking filler cap and padded steering wheel. At the same time the Mini 1000 was fitted with a dipping rear-view mirror, the reclining seats from the Clubman, and a reversing light.

For the 20th birthday of Issigonis' creation, the Mini buyer was offered a special model, the Mini 1100 Special, only available in silver or rose-metallic. It had a vinyl roof and a 15cm-wide graded stripe along the sides. To this were added wheel-arch extensions and rectangular repeater-flashers. The bigger Clubman engine was installed, as were wider tyres on light alloy wheels. The matt black grille had

a polished aluminium surround and the British Leyland badge adorned the bonnet. Inside, the Jubilee Mini was much like the Clubman. There was a three-instrument binnacle directly above the steering column and a centre console containing heating controls, a radio, loudspeaker, clock and cigar lighter.

The occupants sat on attractive check cloth seats with vinyl side panels, and there was a new two-spoke steering wheel with Jubilee badge. Leyland produced 2500 of these special 'eleven hundreds' at a price of £3300, and sold the lot in a few weeks. It was then decided to make the same number again. A similar version, the Super, was available from October 1979.

The policy of producing specials is still maintained to this day. Each one of these was differently equipped, so only the more important models are mentioned here. In September 1980 the City could be had in 1000 and 850 form, and a month later the Super was re-named HL. Until February 1982 there was the Estate, available, like the saloon, with manual or automatic transmission. The Clubman had been quietly dropped. A project to produce a wider version by the simple expedient of cutting the body in half and inserting a 6in/15cm wide strip got nowhere. What had worked for the Minor in 1947 did not provide the answer in the seventies...... The original Mini long outlived the Clubman but received the most useful items of the Clubman's equipment. Up to the Austin Rover re-organization British Leyland were still playing with type designations: City was followed by E, HL was followed by HLE and the latter became the Mayfair in 1982. The Mayfair remained the better equipped variant.

The LAMM Autohaus conversion, which was adopted as the Mini Cabriolet in 1991. It has the chrome Cooper grille and a body kit including flared wheel arches and sill finishers.

The 1275GT had a three-instrument display, a padded dash top rail and the twin air vents of all Mk III models.

In October 1983 there was a Mini series with a famous name, the Sprite, which came with cast-alloy wheels, matt black trim and the 1000cc engine; 2500 were built.

In 1982/3 the van, pick-up and estate models had been discontinued, leaving only the regular production saloon. Limited edition versions of this continued to appear, through to the 1990s, notably the Mini 25 to mark the 25th anniversary in 1984, and the Mini Thirty in 1989. The Mini 25 was based on the Mayfair, and it was followed by others such as the Ritz, in effect a luxury version of the City (1985), the Chelsea (1986), the Park Lane and the Piccadilly, all built in small numbers – 1500-2000 was normal – and for the British market. In 1989 there were two-tone colour schemes, for the Sky and Rose models.

More to the point, by that time the engine had been adapted to use unleaded fuel and by 1991 an exhaust catalyst was available for the City and Mayfair, and the then-new Neon Special Edition (another 1500-off variant, in blue with 'a unique graphics scheme').

Meanwhile there had been colour schemes recalling past glories, on a Mini Racing (dark green with a white roof) and Mini Flame (red with a white roof). The 'real' Mini Cooper had come back, and there was the Mini Thirty. This was a high-specification car, with a clear lacquer application to enhance its pearlescent paintwork and with eight-spoke alloy wheels as well as appropriate badges. The production run was 3000 cars, 400 with a four-speed automatic transmission. The respective maximum speeds were 80mph and 78mph – in that respect performance had not improved much in many years!

Although there had been many independent soft-top conversions, an 'official' convertible did not appear until 1991. In effect one of the German conversions was adopted by Rover as the limited-edition Mini Cabriolet, and its origins were acknowledged in the discreet 'LAMM Design' decals (this German Rover dealer was responsible for the conversion of donor cars produced at Longbridge). Considerable body stiffening was needed, for example with modified sills and a new floor cross member and B posts, and this was coupled with Mini Cooper running gear and a full body styling kit. Initially only 75 were available in 1991, to test the market for increased production in 1992.

The Cabriolet was another variation on the evergreen theme, supplementing the three 'main-line' models, City, Mayfair and Cooper.

Outward differences between the first and second series of the Mini 1275GT were minor.

MINI but not Cooper: The 1275GT

The position of engine and transmission, common to all Minis, is shown in this cutaway sketch of the 1275GT.

The 1275GT arrived in 1969 when the Clubman was introduced and took its place among the rather special Minis: it was something akin to a Cooper S for the family. It weighed 1504lb/683kg, and its 60bhp at 5250rpm gave it a top speed of 87mph; 0-60mph took 13.7 seconds. This was a good three seconds slower than the Cooper 1275S which was still available, but it did have 16 fewer horses than its competition-tried stablemate. The 1275GT was never available in automatic form and its standard equipment included Hydrolastic suspension, servo-assisted braking and a rev counter. Externally, this long-nose model had Rostyle wheels with Dunlop radial tyres and a rally stripe at the bottom edges of the doors; track was just over an inch (3cm) wider in front and 1.5in/4cm wider at the rear compared with other Minis. Through its first two years the 1275GT was barely changed, but when Cooper S production ceased in July 1971, it became the top model in the Mini range. It was then fitted with the rubber suspension, in line with the other models. Modifications for the coming years mostly involved the gearbox, with bearing and synchronization problems which were not finally resolved until 1973. The following

The last version of the 1275GT with Denovo wheels and tyres. The central element in the grille is more prominent and decorated with a horizontal 'Mini' badge. The 'GT' badge had been discarded in 1976.

year saw the installation of a thermostatically controlled flap-valve in the inlet manifold and inertia reel seat belts. Unfortunately at the same time power was reduced to 55bhp (DIN) at 5250rpm; on paper this did not change performance much, but on the road it took some of the engine's bite away.

From August 1974 the 1275GT could be equipped with Denovo wheels and tyres to choice. Dunlop had invested much money in research and even developed a plastic rim together with Citroën – with useful results. However, handling was noticeably influenced by the softer sidewalls, and Denovo tyres did not catch on.

Reclining seats came in 1975, and customers buying the 1275GT in the following year received a much better car: soft, noise-reducing carpets with foam backing, a heated rear screen and ancillary controls on a handy column-mounted stalk were among the improvements. Externally, the '75 model had a different grille with a prominent surround and a badge with the British Leyland logo next to the word Mini.

When in August 1977 the Denovo tyres were fitted as standard, as were tinted windows, no one could guess that these would be the last fundamental improvements to the 1275GT. There were detail enhancements, such as a locking fuel filler cap and reversing lamps, but Mini fans heard warning bells when signals suggesting use of running-out stocks were detected. In October 1979 the 1275GT received the black door mirrors and the black all-round guttering from the Mini production because making special parts for the 1275 was no longer viable – a sure sign of the coming demise of the Clubman range. Those in the know were not surprised to hear the announcement in May 1980 that the 1275GT would not be produced again after the works holidays in August. The 580,000-odd units of all the various Clubman models, including the Estate, seem small beer when measured against the overall success of the Mini – the reason might well be that many Mini customers never quite saw the advantages of the long-nosed car over the original Mini. The Metro that came in the Autumn of 1980 was never really accepted as a successor to the Clubman by the Mini brigade. The loss of the estate car was particularly mourned.

As the Mini Cooper S homologation for front-line competition expired, the 1275GT almost unexpectedly became prominent in British saloon car racing, in a 1275GT one-model series and most notably in the national championship. Entered by a leading dealer, Patrick Motors, Richard Longman won the RAC Saloon Car Championship in 1978-79. This Mini shape also became familiar in rallies and rallycross.

57

MINI Cooper – Giant Killer

This is the innocent appearance of a Cooper in street guise – this is a lhd Mk 1 in Germany.

When the Mini appeared in 1959 it positively screamed to be tuned: it only had the 848cc engine, producing a meagre 34.5bhp at 5500rpm, because the test drivers thought that more performance would be too much for the normal consumer. But in 1959, specialists like Speedwell, Downton and Don Moore descended upon the little Mini. Issigonis did not wholly approve, for he had designed the Mini as a low-price people's car, and it took all of John Cooper's considerable enthusiasm to get an 'official' high-performance version off the ground. Cooper had been using the engine in Formula Junior cars, and one of his thoughts was for a circuit car – rallies do not seem to have figured in his ideas. He converted a car, and after George Harriman, BMC chairman, gave the project his blessing the company took on the development. On every vehicle with the Cooper badge John Cooper received a £2 royalty.

The first Mini-Cooper appeared in September 1961. Its 997cc engine had a 62.4mm bore and 81.2mm stroke, and produced 55bhp at 6000rpm. The increased power resulted not only from the bigger cubic capacity, but also from its sloping twin SU HS2 carburettors. It also had a strengthened crankshaft, a new camshaft, bigger inlet valves and the world's smallest disc brakes. Top speed was 85mph, and the 0-60mph acceleration figure was some 19sec.

In March 1963 a more sporting Cooper S followed – the factory designation was ADO50 – and its cubic capacity of 1071cc was influenced by the 1100cc Formula Junior engine. The Cooper S had an entirely new engine block, the two inner cylinders being closer together by 3.1mm to provide room for a bore of 70.64mm. A nitrided crank for a stroke of 68.26mm was fitted to cope with the increased loading and the long-stroke Mini became the short-stroke Cooper S producing 70bhp at 6000rpm. Bigger brake discs and servo assistance took care of the higher speeds available. As expected, the Mini-Cooper caused quite a stir in racing and rallies – thus three modifications came into being for 1964. In January the 997cc engine made way for the 998 Cooper, and the car was fitted with Hydrolastic

The first Cooper engine in 1961 showing twin SU carburettors with heat shields over the typical three-branch exhaust; the air filters are small. The subframe is identical with the production car but the remote gear change was new.

Flared wheel arches were not a feature of the original Mini-Cooper S Mk I design. The decoration imitates the original racing cars run by John Cooper.

This Morris Mini-Cooper S has been restored to original condition.

A Mini-Cooper S Mk 1 demonstrating the facility on all Minis of carrying large items on the lowered boot lid. The number plate was hinged at the top to allow it to be swung down.

suspension in the autumn of 1969. Then in March 1964 came the big 1275 Cooper – which put 76bhp from 1275cc onto the road. Simultaneously, the smallest Cooper S came onto the market, offering 65bhp at 6500rpm from only 970cc. Because of changed racing rules, the production of the 1071 Cooper S ceased in August 1964. The 970 Cooper S only lived for 11 months – it was dropped in January 1965.

The development of the Mini-Cooper can be summarized as follows: The 997cc (1000) car, in its two-tone paint, with twin carburettors and disc brakes, was introduced in the Autumn of 1961. The disc brakes were developed by Cooper in conjunction with Lockheed, because the

inner rim diameter of barely 8in only left room for 7in drum brakes.

In 1959 John Cooper had got his hands on a pre-production Mini and arranged for racing driver Roy Salvadori to drive it to Italy. He reached Monza quicker than another well-known driver, Reg Parnell, who had left London at the same time driving an Aston Martin DB4GT. This made Cooper think hard about a sporting Mini. The BMC board was soon persuaded – chairman George Harriman needed only a brief test run in a Cooper-modified car – and even Issigonis finally agreed. A small run series of 1000 cars was put in hand, and sold quickly. The Mini-Cooper was adopted as part of the BMC programme. John

The Mini-Cooper S Mk II got the larger rear screen and new rear lights of Mk II Minis, and this is one of the twin-tank cars. All Cooper models could be recognized by their wider wheels with ventilation holes on the S models.

Cooper had already produced a racing version of the A series engine for Formula Junior and sold it, with modest success, but as the basis for a small high-performance road car engine it really made its mark. It gave 70bhp at 6000rpm and could be revved up to 7200. The new block casting had enlarged oilways, fed by a stronger pump. The Lockheed discs got servo assistance and perforated wheels gave better brake cooling.

In January 1964 the 998cc short-stroke twin-carburettor version of the engine from the Riley and Wolseley was used in the Cooper, because its block was 'meatier'.

In March 1964 the new Dunlop SP41 radials were fitted – they improved roadholding considerably. In September 1964 Cooper had to accept the the Hydrolastic suspension, although he was always sceptical of that system. The 1965 Monte Carlo Rally team comprised works cars with and without Hydrolastic. The slight modifications to the clutch and gearbox were also to the benefit of the Cooper series, as was a reclining seat option.

In January 1966 the Mini-Cooper S was fitted with twin fuel tanks and an oil cooler. At the same time the external door handles were changed, because of a terrible accident in the Autumn of 1965 when a schoolchild was killed when its coat caught in the forward facing door handle. The law placed the responsibility for the accident on this 'hook' and Austin Morris had to modify the handle, later using a fixed handle with pushbutton.

In the spring of the same year the Cooper S front suspension was modified with strengthened rubber bushes, while at

The Cooper S engine took up no more space in the engine compartment than the normal unit, but ancillaries such as twin carburettors filled the space, together with a brake servo.

This press photo shows the Austin Cooper S Mk II with the new grille. The little paper sticker above the wiper blade shows that this Austin is exactly the same vehicle as the.....

....Morris Cooper S Mk II which has only the badge to distinguish it.

the rear taper roller bearings were used in the suspension arm mountings. The Cooper programme was included in the changes to the Mk II in October 1967, and during 1968 the new all-synchromesh gearbox was introduced on the Cooper models. Cars with this gearbox had the code letters 'XE' in the engine number prefix. Towards the end of the production run the ways of the Cooper and Cooper S parted. Both received the heated rear window in the Spring of 1969. Cooper Mk II production ceased in November in favour of the 1275GT.

The Cooper S lived on from March 1970 for 16 months as the Mark III, with the new doors and wind-down windows, and the Hydrolastic suspension was dropped towards the end of the run. There was one common feature to the 29,000 Cooper Ss and the 98,000 Coopers: none of them had a rev counter as standard....

Changes to the competition Mini-Cooper are described in the chapter on rallies – here is a short overview of the street versions:

In September 1961 the Austin and Morris Cooper with 997cc engine came onto the market, built at Longbridge. High performance resulted mainly from twin carburettors and better braking from the smallest disc brakes in the world.

In March 1963 the Mini-Cooper S was launched, still in Austin or Morris guise. Its short-stroke engine derived from the BMC A block and gave 70bhp at 6000rpm. The bigger and better disc brakes of the Cooper S were of 7½ inch diameter.

In 1964 the short-stroke Cooper appeared with the Riley/Wolseley 998cc engine, producing 55bhp at 5800rpm and an ideal basis for performance tuning. The 998 took the place of the original Cooper after some 25,000 vehicles had been made and remained in production until 1969.

Two sister models were added to the first 1071cc Cooper S in March 1964. One was the potent 970 S with 65bhp at a high 6500rpm from the short-stroke engine and the other the long-stroke 1275 S with 76bhp at 5800rpm. The 970cc version was developed particularly for British saloon car racing and homologated in the under 1000cc class. All 972 examples were produced in 1964 and '65 and the 970 S is extremely rare today, perhaps because many were 'used up' in motor sport events.

Altogether 4016 units of the 1071 version left the line at Longbridge in 1963/64. All Cooper models were fitted with Hydrolastic from late 1964, even though racing teams and tuners were not happy with this suspension.

The previously mentioned 1275 S replaced the 1071 S (only built until the end of 1964) and over seven years a production total of 24,000 was reached. This car achieved outstanding success in rallying and as a Group I racer. For homologation purposes, standard production cars received a second fuel tank in the opposite rear corner and an oil cooler. Apart from this the Cooper 998 and 1275 S from 1965 were subject to the same modifications as the 'regular' Minis; as a result and from October 1967 the Mk II versions had the new grille, larger rear window and different rear lamps.

A Mk I Morris Mini-Cooper poses with ladies. 55bhp from 998cc at 5800rpm provided quite enough power for everyday motoring.

This red Cooper S with its black roof won concours prizes in the 1980s. Here it is displayed with a trophy in 1985.

For restoration purists, a chromed and polished engine is not a real goal, but an ultra-clean engine, here a Cooper S, can be pleasing. The big, chromed oil filter at top left is of course not original.

The 998cc Mini-Cooper was dropped at the end of 1969, leaving the field free for the 1275, which was built until June 1971. In the last year it was fitted also with the new doors with wind-up windows and from then on was known simply as Mini-Cooper S, without Austin or Morris badges.

The Innocenti Mini-Cooper 1300 provided a real sporting Mini for some Continental markets. Externally it was recognizable by its quarter lights, side repeaters and a new company logo on the grille. Internally it had sports seats and a well-equipped dashboard.

Total Mini-Cooper production between 1961 and 1969 was around 98,000, while almost 29,000 Mini Cooper Ss were built 1963-71. Both were available with Austin or Morris badges, and in both cases almost two-thirds were badged as Morris owing to Morris cars being more popular in export markets, especially Australia, where the Mini-Coopers were assembled from CKD kits. The Mk III Cooper S was badged as a Mini-Cooper.

Meanwhile in some Continental countries there was more enthusiasm for the Innocenti Cooper 1300S than for the 1275 GT. The former was very attractively equipped, but not available in the UK. *Auto-Zeitung* of Cologne tested one, and found it capable of over 100mph with acceleration to 62mph in 11.3 seconds. They wrote: 'without undue euphoria, but factually and soberly we must state that this vehicle is really created for today's economic situation.....it is the ideal town car, equally usable for long distances, economic to operate and, on top of this, provides any amount of driving fun....'

The Cooper legend did not fade with time, and the hot hatchbacks it inspired – VW Golf GTi, Peugeot 205GTi, Ford Escort XR3i, and others – only confirmed that the market did not vanish when a dull-witted management decision killed the Mk III in 1971. John Cooper was well aware of this, years later marketing an 'Anniversary' version of the City model, and selling performance

conversions to Japan from his Sussex garage. The Anniversary version had engine maximum power increased from 48bhp to 64bhp, and outwardly it was distinguished by stripes and decals. It evoked the feel of the old Cooper, without any pretence that it was a 'new Cooper'. Meanwhile, the continuing demand for a high-performance version was shown by the reception for the Mini Turbo developed by ERA Limited.

The two strands came together as Rover Cars, direct successors to BMC in this respect, reintroduced the Mini-Cooper in July 1990. This was developed in association with John Cooper and ERA, and in many ways was hardly 're-packaged'.

The engine was a 1275cc A series unit with an exhaust catalyst fitted as standard. This developed 61bhp at 5500rpm, and the new Cooper covered 0-60mph in 11.2 sec and had a top speed of 92mph/148kmh (the earlier model had 76bhp, giving respective figures of 10.6sec and 97mph/155.5kmh).

The initial batch of 1000 had leather interior trim, a glass sun roof, auxiliary driving lights and wheel arch extensions with alloy road wheels. A 'Special Edition' version had more luxurious interior treatment. The first batch of cars had white bonnet stripes, and carried John Cooper's signature.

After such a long interval, it was launched without a mark number, and in no way 'devalued' the earlier cars cherished by collectors. Nonetheless, it was welcomed by enthusiasts for Mini motoring, not least in Japan.

In 1991 John Cooper Garages introduced a performance kit to resurrect the S, and provided the conversion was carried out by Cooper Garages or a Rover dealer it was covered by a full warranty.

It comprised the fitment of twin SU HS2 carburettors, a new cylinder head with gas-flowed inlet and exhaust ports, a new inlet manifold and a centre-branch exhaust manifold. That improved the power output of the 1275cc A series engine from 61bhp in standard Mini Cooper form to 78bhp at 6000rpm – or some 110bhp/ton – while maximum torque was increased from 67lb/ft to 78lb/ft at a relatively low 3250rpm. Conversions from mainstream Mini-Coopers also need an oil cooler (the Special Edition version had one as standard). Coopers also offered a handling pack, including Koni adjustable shock absorbers, and items such as a clamp to lower the steering column.

In outright performance terms, the 'S' was just a 100mph car (Coopers claimed that as its maximum speed) but in less measurable qualities such as responsiveness and feel the 32-year-old design was a match for its early-1990s small 'GT' contemporaries.

Downton Engineering

Any discussion of tuned Minis must include Daniel Richmond's efforts, for he believed in the sporting potential of the Mini just as strongly as John Cooper. But Richmond confined himself to tuning and modifications only against specific orders. He had no engineering department, but possessed an incredible inventiveness, tantamount to genius. His small workshops had been set up to undertake restoration work on Bugattis and Lagondas. The company was named Downton Engineering for its geographical location and Richmond called his cars Downton-Minis; the commercial management was in the hands of his wife Bunty.

His first sports Mini was on its wheels as early as the end of 1959 and Downton was soon known as a good address for reliable sports Minis. George Harriman of BMC and Alec Issigonis were good friends, and so were Alex Moulton, BMC competitions manager Stuart Turner, John Cooper and Charles Griffin. This apart, Richmond was one of the clique which had formed around Issigonis and he frequently received tuning commissions from Longbridge. Unfortunately Richmond was very reserved and only known to the cognoscenti – but they recognized his abilities and used to say in jest that his engines were always so clean because he shared his gin with them. More seriously, he was not inclined to discuss exactly what he did to the engines, but his bored-out 1088cc cars were genuine 100mph machines.

When the rally Mini had passed its zenith at the end of the 1960s and the British club racing scene turned to increasingly wild conversions with Ford BDA and hot Imp engines, Richmond lost interest in Mini tuning and turned towards the 1100 and the big 1800. He only modified Mini engines if specialists like Crayford, Radford or Wood & Pickett had a rich customer who asked for a bit more performance.....

The carburettor-engined 1990 Mini-Cooper was replaced in 1991 by the fuel-injected Mini-Cooper 1.3i, photographed here in the pits at Goodwood race circuit with John Cooper.

Daniel Richmond of Downton Engineering was a tuner in the classic mould. Here he proudly displays his cylinder heads and manifolds. For many years, the Downton Minis from his works were much sought after and reliable sporting machines.

Richmond supported successful drivers, giving them contracts which provided the car, service and parts from Downton. This is John Fitzpatrick in May 1964 at Mallory Park in the 1300cc class; he won, beating the Broadspeed cars by a good margin.

Downton Engineering had a lot of well-known customers, like the Aga Khan, the German Prince Metternich, Steve McQueen, the Formula I driver Dan Gurney and Lord Snowdon who loved the cars. Even Enzo Ferrari used a Downton-Mini when he wanted a change from conventional cars – he had been friendly with Issigonis for years.

There is an amusing littly story about Downton and Enzo Ferrari. During an Italian visit Richmond and Issigonis agreed to present Ferrari with an automatic Mini. Richmond drove the beautifully prepared car to Modena, accompanied by his wife, and was a little surprised that there was a degree of reserve when the present was accepted: despite all the enthusiasm, the men at Downton had forgotten to modify a left-hand-drive car.

Sadly Richmond died early, when he was only 46. His wife ran the businesss for another five years and ended the firm's activities with a tragic act: one morning her housekeeper came in to find a note saying that she would find her employer dead in the adjoining room. Before committing suicide Bunty had closed the books. When they found her farewell letter, it asked that the first car modified by her husband, UHR 850, which the Richmonds had always kept as an exhibition piece, was either to be exhibited in a museum by their friend Charles Griffin or destroyed by fire....

Fortunately the Heritage Museum was just being opened and the Richmond car, which had made its racing debut at Spa, can be seen today alongside the first production Mini-Minor, the Twinny-Mini, Aaltonen's Monte-winning car of 1967, a Michelotti prototype and other prototypes.

Rover's 1990 Mini Cooper with a 1960s version

Twinny MINI – There's No Moke without Fire

Twin tracks in the snow – the Mighty-Moke demonstrated in the harsh winter of 1963 how well a vehicle with four driven wheels could perform. Jack Daniels is the driver, with a load of straw bales. This experimental vehicle had a 948cc engine at the front and an 848cc unit at the rear. In the picture below, Issigonis is the passenger.

This is the military version with two 1100cc engines, prepared for tests by the US Army, who did not buy it.

Early in 1963 Alec Issigonis rang his friend John Cooper and invited him to see his new toy; a Moke with a 950cc engine in front and an 850cc unit at the rear, and to test it in deep snow. After this impressive 'play-time' weekend they persuaded BMC to invite the Press to Longbridge while there was still snow on the ground. Journalists did not need to be asked twice and they saw not only the new, yet to be announced Moke, but a twin-engined one to boot. To demonstrate its possible use, they roared through the snow, the rear loaded with straw, perhaps so as not to divulge the final shape.

The enthusiasm of the journalists encouraged Issigonis and Cooper (two men with but a single thought) to build a Twinny-Mini from a Mini. Instead of working together, they worked in friendly competition. A few weeks later Cooper's Twinny was ready, one day before Issigonis' Longbridge team's effort. Sir John Whitmore, a well known saloon car racer, drove the car at Brands Hatch, and due to less than 100 percent engine synchronization it made a peculiar noise like a V8. At last one could drift a Mini, accelerating out of the corners on four powered wheels! From April two tuned Cooper engines were producing a full 175bhp between them, from 2½ litres.

Whitmore tried to persuade BMC to build a Twinny-Mini for the famous many-cornered Targa Florio, run over a sinuous road circuit in Sicily – they were actually talked into it and ordered two Downton engines. Soon Whitmore and the well-known journalist and racing driver Paul Frère were practising in Sicily on the 70km mountain circuit. In those days it was thought that 3 days and 20 laps would suffice to memorize the 700 bends and corners; official practice times showed a remarkable 47mins 11sec for the Twinny while the normal Downton car needed a good 50 minutes. Although Downton had done an excellent job for BMC, particularly regarding the gear selection for both engines, the Twinny remained a treacherous beast. It also suffered from increasing cooling problems and these put paid to its racing debut. The Mini stopped after each lap to take on water, the simultaneous driver change

Twinny-Moke with two 1100cc engines. Although performance was good military experts could not accept a vehicle that offered so little space and load capacity.

The air intakes of the rear engine, and the huge fuel tank, can be seen through the open 'boot lid' of this prototype

being simply a diversionary tactic. After a fast lap of 48 min Whitmore stopped at the pits, staying in the car since the rear temperature gauge showed normal; he roared off – only to switch off the rear engine after two kilometres because it had overheated. A slow 55 min lap resulted,

The Twinny idea was attractive to independent special builders. Paul Emery was behind this 1965 effort; it had two modified engines and the combined output claimed was 236bhp.

while the ordinary Mini made it in 51 min. The Twinny was simply under-developed.

The first thing to be seen under the boot lid with its two large triangular air inlets was an enormous fuel tank (it held at least 100 litres) restrained by two straps. Above the tank on the right a cardboard air intake was fitted, next to it the two round air filters for the Weber carburettors. The engine fitted into the available space just as it was; later, a makeshift fibreglass cover was installed. Exhaust pipes protruded behind each wheel.

After the Targa Florio debâcle Longbridge was relieved not to have entered the car built by Issigonis; George Harriman strictly forbade Charles Griffin to enter the car in races because it was potentially dangerous. He might well have realized how much excess power the little bolide possessed. John Cooper was to experience this, at the cost of considerable agony. Cooper at that time was also a very successful constructor of racing cars of world-wide repute. The twin-engined prototype was at the Cooper works, and John was driving it from Fairoaks (where a pilot had taxied into his light aircraft) to a dinner with Roy Salvadori when he crashed heavily on the Kingston Bypass. The car rolled several times, and Cooper suffered concussion and cracked ribs. The car was heavily damaged, and Cooper had no recollection of the accident, so a precise cause could not be pinpointed. One theory blamed the redundant steering arms at the rear, which were simply welded onto the chassis frame via a link, to stop the rear wheels from steering. One of the steering arms broke, it was suggested, a wheel suddenly angled to the right and the car rolled. It was also suggested that the twin transmissions slipped out of harmony. Either way, the Twinny was a write off.

Longbridge made considerable efforts to interest the British and US armies in an air-portable military forerunner of the Moke, as a lightweight utility that could be dropped by parachute. Its lack of four-wheel drive proved to be a major shortcoming – there were others, such as its small wheels – so a 'Twinny-Moke' was offered with two 1100cc engines and transmission linked through a common gear lever. A major drawback was the lack of goods or personnel space, as there was only a small high platform above the rear engine. No armies took it up. A prototype with two 848cc engines is preserved in running order in the Heritage Museum.

The story of push-and-pull Minis ended with two racing drivers who tried their luck on British circuits with 1500cc Ford engines and 'Mini-Jaguar' adaptations. They were not successful.

MINI-Moke, for Beach or Boulevard

The new Mini-Moke in 1964.

On the face of it all the world's armies needed a small, all-terrain vehicle, light enough to be lifted by helicopter and parachuted, and in the case of the Moke designed so that several vehicles could be stacked one on top of another. However the Moke's small wheels were a problem, as was its limited ground clearance and lack of traction in certain conditions. For civilian use in the UK the Moke was tax-rated as a car and not a van, which restricted its acceptance as a second vehicle. In warm climates the Moke served as a taxi, fun car, or light pick up, ideal for the beach, golf, private yacht or as a shopping car. For that one front engine sufficed and so the series-production version was announced in March 1964, fitted with the standard 848cc engine, although its direct military predecessor had seen the light of day in March 1962, and the earliest prototype more than two years before that.

The Moke had the rubber suspension used on the Countryman and Traveller, whilst the subframes for the front and rear suspension were bolted to the steel monocoque box frame. The angular shape of the military prototype and the fold-flat screen were retained. A simple hood and frame gave the passengers some protection. They also had a grab-handle each and the instruments came from the 850 Mini; left- and right-hand drive versions were listed. British production ended in October 1968, barely 4 years after manufacture had begun – 14,518 were made and only 1467 remained in the UK; all the others were exported. After production ended in the UK, the tooling was transferred to Australia and some were later made in Portugal to the end of the 1970s when a further 22,507 units had been manufactured and sold. From the end of 1984 Mokes were built again, to order only, by the Portuguese subsidiary of Austin Rover. Production was resumed on a commercial basis in Portugal early in 1991, by Moke Automobili (Portugal) Automovils LDA, part of the Italian Cagiva Group.

The basis of all Mokes was the the Mini engine, transmission, front suspension and driving compartment 'module', and the early military prototypes leading to the Twinny Moke (but nobody liked this twin-engined concept). It had the 848cc engine and although it did not become popular with the motoring public in Britain it caught on in other countries – some of the original little cars can still be seen in Cyprus, in Spain and elsewhere where it is sunny.

The Moke was also very popular among producers of TV programmes. All in white, with a red and white striped top, it enlivened the long-running series 'The Prisoner', and in a comedy series about animals it transported the giraffe Tiny with its neck sticking through a round hole in a white-and-yellow top. It played small roles in many British, French and Italian films.

Officially and until the end of its production in October 1968, the Moke was fitted only with the small engine and 10in wheels. The potential market was probably over-estimated by Austin – 14,518 units is hardly a viable number in four years of production – especially as only 1467 of these were sold on the British market.

Australian production – which started after a pause of two years – was more successful, and a few vehicles were even exported to the UK. Externally it had 12in wheels, different flashers and a modified folding top. Some 22,500 units were produced, which made a total, including the Portugese licence manufacture, of some 37,100 units.

For some time the Portugese Moke could be bought in England, called Californian. After BL Australia had sold the production tooling to Portugal, kit-car maker Tim Dutton imported some into the UK, naming these 'Moke Californian'. As the 1990s opened a specialist dealer, Duncan Hamilton, imported used examples to meet a steady cult demand.

The Moke that was put back into production in the same Portugese factory in 1991 was substantially modified. It was still powered by the A series engine, rated at 39bhp at 4750rpm and using lead-free fuel. A full roll cage was fitted (the Dutton cars had featured a prominent roll-over bar), front and rear bull bars were standard, 12in wheels were fitted, the soft top was simpler and more effective in weather-protection terms, and there was a small locking luggage compartment. The bodywork was fully galvanized.

Duncan Hamilton, the UK concessionaire, offered utility and SE versions. The SE had 'eight-spoke' alloy wheels, tinted screen glass, and lesser accessories that tended to emphasize the fun or outdoor sport uses for the Moke rather than the utilitarian purposes behind its 30-year-old origins. And the word 'Mini' was nowhere to be found on the vehicle or in the literature...

A Frankfurt-registered Mini-Moke with trailer, and a full load of accessories.

There was a Moke in the UK again from 1984, built in Portugal. Imports were handled by Tim Dutton, then a kit-car maker in Sussex; and the price was about £4400. He called it Moke Californian and fitted roo and roll-over bars, wide wheels and sports seats.

In most respects the 1991 Portugese version of the Moke followed the early-1980s models. This is the SE, with 'eight-spoke' wheels and sump guard, as well as the sturdy bull bar.

As a small load carrier, the Moke was very popular in Australia. In 1977 an Australian Moke was even entered for the prestigious London-Sydney rally.

This short-wheelbase prototype did not go into series production.

◄ The Ant derivative with four-wheel drive. About 25 units were produced during 1967 for evaluation by various armies world wide, but no orders resulted. Several survivors are known to exist including one in the Heritage Museum.

MINI Goes Rallying

The history of the Austin/Morris works rally team roughly falls into three parts after the first private efforts. There were modest beginnings under the leadership of Marcus Chambers, replaced in 1960 by the ambitious Stuart Turner, under whose aegis the great Monte Carlo victories were won. At the end of 1966, when BMC became British Motor Holdings, Turner left and his place was taken by Peter Browning.

The Background

Even in Cecil Kimber's Morris Garages days MGs were prepared for competition. Abingdon's modern competition department dated from 1954, initially under Syd Enever, which was responsible for MG development, modifying customers' cars and competition. Due to the increasing work load caused by the development of the MGA a proper competitions manager, Marcus Chambers, was appointed: he had had considerable mechanical and racing experience pre-war. He was one of those Englishmen who love good food and vintage wines.

To support him Doug Watts joined the department: formerly a Riley tester, he was to be team chief and 'coach' to the future works team. To cope with homologation problems Chambers recruited a young businessman, Bill Price, who later managed quite a few competition entries by himself. A description of the times when the team was not exactly over-burdened with winning potential in the shape of the Magnette, MGA and Austin A90, is beyond the scope of this book. The story of the competition Minis, starting in the late summer of 1959, is our subject here.

When the first Mini 850 appeared in the competition department Doug Watts refused to drive it to the bank, embarrassed to be seen in such an insignificant little car. There is still no agreement about who was first to recognize the rallying potential of the Mini. As early as 1959 Pat Moss and Stuart Turner won a club event by almost ten minutes, but after winning this Mini Miglia run by the Knowldale Automobile Club, Pat Moss thought the Mini too slow and Turner pronounced it particularly uncomfortable.

Women had long been drivers of BMC works cars. Pat Moss, for instance, battled valiantly in the Monte in an Austin Healey 3000 and was to win the Liège-Rome-Liège in a 'big Healey'. Pat Ozanne was a member of the 1959 RAC Rally works team, joining Alick Pitts and Ken James. All three Minis dropped out because of a trifling fault, as faulty oil seals led to clutch slip – even scientific application of the powder contents of fire extinguishers did not help. In those days the co-driver's role was a relatively minor one. Only when young Tony Ambrose, a student from Oxford, joined the team, did matters change. He introduced the predecessor of today's 'bible'.

The first major international effort was the Monte Carlo Rally of 1960. Alongside the works teams with tuned cars, three drivers started with production cars, among them a team consisting of Nancy Mitchell and Tish Ozanne. The clutch problem was still unresolved and for Pitts and Ambrose this meant sand in the clutch as well as the fire-extinguisher powder. This resulted in a solid clutch, unwilling to separate, but the Mini bombed on, and in thick fog in the Massif Central it ran at high speed into the back of another competitor, damaging the

The first rally entries were completely independent, and in 1959 the cars were driven by private owners and were absolutely standard, even down to the 850cc engine.

The 1961 Monte team outside the gates at Abingdon. Left to right: TMO 559 with Peter Garnier and Rupert Jones (they collided with a privately driven car), Tom Christie and Ninian Paterson with TMO 560 (they suffered food poisoning). Derek Astle and Steve Woolley (TMO 561) hit a rock, but this car was later driven to a Tulip Rally class win.

radiator and bending the left rear wheel out of track in the ensuing pirouette. The service crew carried out a makeshift repair but it did not last long: Pitts rammed a stand with milk churns during the next stage and totalled the car in a river of creamy milk. Without a single piece of glass and with doors tied shut, TMO 560 reached Monte Carlo, where the team explained to the amazed organizers that they wished to drive their heap of scrap in the final mountain test. Yet again makeshift repairs enabled the car to take part in this last elimination test and, helped by much sand and a few stops to collect fallen off bits, it finished in 73rd position. Its unlucky driver, Alick Pitts, is said to have offered his team chief Marcus Chambers 10 shillings for the mortal remains of the works car. Meanwhile other Minis had finished 23rd, 33rd and 55nd.

The first class win in an International was secured when the Morley twins, Don and Erle, won their class in the Swiss Geneva Rally. Don was small and lively, Erle tall and quiet – they always started in immaculately clean and pressed clothes. BMC participated in all the important rallies in 1960 and the 850cc TMO 561 won its class in the Alpine Rally. TMO 561 had served as a works car since 1959 and did duty until May 1961; then the red car with its white roof was sold to Ann Wisdom. The first two works cars TMO 559 and TMO 560 were sold for symbolic sums by way of rewards to Vic Elford (TMO 559), TMO 560 to Pitts. Before being sold, TMO 561 scored yet another class win in the 1961 Tulip Rally. The Monte Carlo Rally of that year saw all three cars drop out. Thus ended the rally history of the 850cc works cars, proving that despite their clutch and shock absorber problems, and the small wheels, they had the stuff of which rally cars are made. For 1962 the new 997cc cars plus a new competition manager were at the ready.

The Coopers

John Cooper was to be responsible for the works team on the circuits, while his name was carried to the rally forefront by the team managed by Stuart Turner. Coopers were internationally known as constructors of single-seater racing cars, and as far as BMC equipment was concerned had adapted the A series engine for Formula Junior cars, bored out to 994cc to give some 75-80bhp in 1961. This engine was to be rated at 70bhp in the first rallying (997cc) Mini Coopers, and it was to prove very reliable.

Marcus Chambers left his successor a well-ordered house with qualified mechanics, good drivers and useful co-drivers. He was particularly proud of having signed up with the fast Scandinavians Rauno Aaltonen and Timo Makinen, who were very quick on snow and gravel. Stuart Turner managed not only the Mini teams but also the successful Austin Healey 3000s. He gave the new Mini Coopers their first outing in the Monte Carlo Rally. Due to hasty preparation the results were somewhat thin; the works team also lost one of the cars in spectacular fashion.

While in second position behind Erik Carlsson, Aaltonen crashed into a wall on the Col di Turini; the car somersaulted and caught fire. Despite serious burns, co-driver Geoff Mabbs pulled the unconscious Aaltonen

Tommy Gold and Mike Hughes won their class with TMO 561 in the Coupe des Alpes of 1960.

The works 997cc cars started a great run of success: Pat Moss and Ann Wisdom won the ladies cup in three 1962 rallies, here at Monte Carlo.

TMO 560 in the 1960 Coupe des Alpes driven by Alick Pitts and Tony Ambrose.

months in which to prepare new vehicles.

Paddy Hopkirk joined the team for 1963: he was to prove a good choice, becoming one of the most successful Mini pilots of all time. Another lady also joined, Val Domleo; she and Pauline Mayman became a new pairing after Pat Moss went over to Ford.

The 1963 season began auspiciously for the Mini-Cooper with third and sixth places overall in the Monte Carlo Rally, and then in the Dutch event a second and a class win. The Alpine in June brought another breakthrough: the mixed double of Rauno Aaltonen and Ann Ambrose won a Coupe des Alpes. A new car was responsible for this success, the 1071cc Cooper S had made its impressive debut.

Customers could buy the 1071cc (70bhp at 6000rpm) Mini-Cooper S from March 1963 and even in production form it could exceed 95mph, although it was somewhat heavier at 635 kilos. The short-stroke engine (70.6 x 68.26mm) revved freely and its reliability persuaded BMC to change over to the new Cooper S during the season. This gave them a third place overall in the Tour de France and a fourth in the RAC Rally at the end of the year. In both cases the Paddy Hopkirk/Henry Liddon team was responsible.

from the vehicle, which was a write off. Rauno recalled later that 'everything was peaceful and warm' when Mabbs' loud voice brought him to, yelling at him and with the car resting on its roof, dragging him out by the armpits into the freezing weather outside. The Pat Moss/Ann Wisdom pairing finished 26th overall and 7th in class, as well as winning the Coupe de Dames. In the Tulip Rally they improved by winning outright in the Mini Cooper 737 ABL – the first win in a major event for the little red and white box. After this success Ann Wisdom retired from motor sport and married rally and racing driver Peter Riley.

Other major European rallies were also contested in 1962, when the most successful car remained 737 ABL, winning the Baden Baden and Geneva events outright. Pauline Mayman proved her qualities as co-driver in place of Tony Ambrose, and later this charming Midlands housewife turned out to be an exceptional driver as well.

The Mini Cooper shows its teeth

The regular rally year has opened with the Monte Carlo for decades, and the Paris-Dakar contest does not really change that, as it is a non-championship one-off. Thus, from the end of the RAC rally in November, there are two

The flying Finn, Rauno Aaltonen (with Tony Ambrose), on the way to a class win in the 1964 Coupe des Alpes.

Tough test. 272 MOX survived this hard landing during tests on a military proving ground in England.

It is often argued that rally victories were not directly reflected in sales but during the Tour de France the BMC dealer in Montpelier announced that he had taken nine orders for the new Cooper S and the dealer in Paris re-ordered three times his yearly quota! The customers seemed impressed that the little Minis were able to see off the big Ford Falcon Sprints, let alone Mercedes and Citroëns.

David and Goliath: Mini wins the Monte

The Monte Carlo Rally has traditionally started from several European cities, mainly because the drive through different countries brings publicity. In 1964 Hopkirk and Liddon started from Minsk in Russia and had the toughest route ahead to the start of the Route Commune (at Rheims that year). Due to poor signposting they lost their way several times and stopped once, after a 180 degree turn right in front of a scowling soldier who, without any hesitation, lifted his rifle.

In France too there were anxious moments for the pair: roaring the wrong way down a one-way street a gendarme stepped into the road, stopped them, and asked for their log book to note their traffic contravention, which would

certainly have disqualified them. Brazenly, Hopkirk explained that he had abandoned the rally because he needed to go to the funeral of a close relative and that was the reason why he was in such a hurry. This seemed almost plausible: the suspicious gendarme noted their names and the car's registration and grudgingly let them go. Paddy would have given a lot to see the policeman's face some time later when he saw that a certain Monsieur Hopkirk in Mini Cooper S 33 EJB had won the Monte Carlo Rally outright.

The other team cars finished fourth and seventh overall (Makinen and Aaltonen), enough for a second and third in their class: only the ladies team was unlucky: Mayman/Domleo pirouetted on sheet ice and damaged 277 EBL beyond repair.

After the Monte the team contested the Tulip and won outright. In the Coupe des Alpes fourth and sixth positions almost seemed a poor return, but the Coupe des Dames fell to the unlucky Monte pair. The team also repeated a Monte success, winning the prize for the best works team. The rest of the year went badly: the new Cooper 1275 was not reliable enough and suffered a series of failures. Indeed in November 1964 there was disaster when all four works cars retired in the RAC Rally. Yet the 1275 had provided

The 1964 rally season saw Minis gain much prestige, with the Dutch Tulip Rally and the Coupe des Alpes, and above all the Monte. Above: Paddy Hopkirk and Henry Liddon with the Cooper S on their way to victory in the winter classic. Below: The pair collecting their rewards.

such hope in March 1964, because the same engine block could at last be used for both 1300 and 1000cc classes. The extra cubic capacity resulted from a different crankshaft which made the smaller and lower powered (by 7bhp) engine into a long-stroke 1275cc unit.

The unreliability of the new Cooper 1275S was mitigated by a brilliant run in the most challenging long-distance event of that time, from the Belgian town of Spa to Sofia in Bulgaria and back to Liège. No Mini had finished in the Spa-Sofia-Liège before 1964 – thus it was a singular success when Wadsworth/Wood brought their Cooper S 570 FMO into 20th place overall.

Immediately afterwards four cars competed in the Tour de France, but only the ladies team (Pauline Mayman and Val Domleo) got to the finish, winning their class. Their team colleagues either dropped out or were unlucky, as in the case of Timo Makinen and his new co-pilot Paul Easter. The latter stood in for Don Barrow, who was ill, but the young garage owner from Stratford had little rally experience. His baptism of fire came quickly in his first major event: between stages he took the wheel to give Makinen a chance to rest. They were well placed

when a car shot out of a side street in Grenoble and so startled Easter that he swerved, bounced off the pavement and then totalled the car. Makinen woke up, got out of the wreck and said to the horrified Easter: 'See to it that we find a decent bar so you can buy me a drink....' There was no further talk about the accident. The end of their Tour de France made for the beginning of a long partnership and friendship between Makinen and Easter, proving that two contrasting characters could form a balanced team for future successes.

Minis dominant

The 1965 season saw BMC more heavily committed to the rally programme than ever. From January to September not one month went by without an international event, and in July there were four: first the Czechoslovakia Rally, then the Nordrhein-Westfalen, the Coupe des Alpes and, at the end of the month, the strenuous Polish event. While the teams changed around, the attendants and service crews sweated long and hard throughout.

The first of the 12 events of this great rallying year presented the cars and their drivers with extremely wintry conditions; the '65 Monte was run in a welter of snow. Makinen and Easter started from Stockholm. Even on the early stages the roads were snowy, and then there were snow storms in France. Other competitors may have proceeded slowly and carefully towards the first elimination test, but Timo really forced his car on. Spikes were beginning to be used and the Finn made full use of them, reckoning that the Mini's limited ground clearance meant that he could 'toboggan' along whilst retaining traction.

Conditions were positively Siberian on the first stages. Many of the cars' electric systems became overloaded, for all lights, heated screens and windscreen wipers were in constant use. In fearsome conditions only 35 of the 237 starters managed to qualify for the elimination test. Others lost their way, became stuck in snow, had electrical problems or went off – arriving within the time limit was near-impossible. Makinen was the only driver to reach Monte Carlo without loss of a single penalty point for lateness, and he had made best time in three of the five special tests. The Mini simply became a snow plough and battled through drifts – Makinen said it 'swam' on the snow to the finish line.

Now the 35 teams who qualified for the Mountain Circuit were faced by the famous 680 kilometres over the Alpes Maritimes, including the Col di Turini. Several different car designs seemed to be in contention for leadership: the Citroën DS with its hydropneumatic suspension and smooth underside driven by Lucien Bianchi, the rear-engined Porsche 911R of Eugen Böhringer, the front-wheel drive Saab 96 of Pat Moss, the 'traditional' Sunbeam Tiger of Peter Harper, and the light Mini, which led by ten minutes. Timo set his sights high right from the start; his motto was 'flat out, stay awake and maximum safety'. This seemed to pay until the middle of the night when the distributor contact spring broke, jeopardizing their win. Mini drivers are well aware that the distributor is not very accessible, particularly on the Monte car, where the cap was screwed down and protected by a rubber hood. After

Makinen and Easter driving to their overall win in the 1965 Monte Carlo Rally.

a few minutes Paul and Timo had found the trouble. They fitted new contacts in all of four(!) minutes – in the dark – a time any specialized workshop would consider terrific, and went on with their victory drive in the now famous Mini Cooper 1275S with the registration AJB 44B and start number 52. They were still 4.5 minutes quicker over the stages than any other team. Two other Cooper Ss made it to the finish line in 26th and 27th position, Hopkirk/Liddon taking a class win and the Morley twins second in their class.

Journalists in London might well have been astonished had they known what the winning pair discovered on the evening of the prize-giving. Prince Rainier and Princess Grace of Monaco noticed that Timo and Paul were late for the official prize-giving. As was then customary they wanted to drive the winning car to the palace. Attired in smart suits they got into the Mini, but AJB 44B would not start. Mechanic Nobby Hall was called and a defect discovered that might have cost them their win. When they had distributor trouble during the night, they forgot the washer insulating the contacts from the distributor housing, yet during the whole of the test the contact stayed on its pivot without touching the base plate! Timo and Paul arrived late and with dirty fingernails for the victory celebrations.

In February the Rally circus travelled to Sweden, but, apart from the Monte-winning car, the Mini team took new cars. All fell victim to the cold, when thickened oil caused the differentials to fail due to lack of lubrication.

Hopkirk and Harryman took over the car which Aaltonen and Ambrose had used in the 1964 RAC for the Circuit of Ireland. This time all went well and the 1275S, CRX 89B, won against a determined bunch of Cortina crews.

The Tulip was another very wintry rally and Timo and Paul were again at the wheel of their Monte Carlo car. Other teams had not reckoned on the snow and conditions became so bad that several special stages had to be cancelled. Makinen coaxed the Mini into third overall and a class win, even though the organizers tried to split the classes differently. Don Morley's Austin Healey 3000 made it into second place.

In May the team travelled to Greece, where Timo and Paul had DJB 93B for the Acropolis Rally. This was a chapter of accidents. First they lost their exhaust – no time for repairs. On the next stage there was a smell of burning – exhaust gases had so heated the floor that the carpets caught fire. That was no reason for Timo to stop, and as the Mini rushed through the stage burning pieces of carpet were thrown from its windows. When Makinen and Easter reached the Peloponnese ferry, they found that the rubber bushes of the subframes had to be renewed. Aboard the ferry, they laid the car on its side and began to dismantle the drive shafts. Petrol leaked from the left fuel tank filler and ran into the bilges – via the ship's ventilation. A smell of petrol spread and a furious officer stopped further work. After the ferry docked, the car was pushed off and laid over on its side again, this time on straw. Repairs completed, back on the route and again in the lead, the pair discovered that the rear subframe had broken. On top of this the rough Greek roads caused a hole in the sump and the rear wheels, hitting the body, began to disintegrate. At the next service point welding was necessary, and following usual Mini practice the car was again tipped on its left side. Again fuel leaked out, a welding spark fell into it and in seconds the car was in flames. Timo leaned in at least to rescue his money and passport. Helpers brought the flames under control. Repairs completed, the car rejoined the 14 competitors that were left. But a damaged carburettor caused rough running and finally the 1275cc engine gave up with bearing trouble. Timo and Paul sat in the sun and waited in vain for the service car, whilst the other competitors roared past; in the meantime Stuart Turner had written off the service barge in a collision!

Further successes followed in June and July 1965 when Aaltonen/Ambrose won the Geneva Rally and, in another car, the Czech event. The Coupe des Alpes was the next major event, and the four Mini crews won a total of 27 cups, perhaps the biggest number of 'pots' ever amassed in one event by a works team. Three Alpine cups went to the Mini drivers Hopkirk, Makinen and Fall, and Hopkirk was delighted with his silver cup for finishing three times without loss of penalty points. The Coupe des Dames in the touring car class narrowly fell to a Mini for the third time running. Pauline Mayman and Val Domleo had a slipping fan belt and the radiator boiled. They stopped by a mountain stream to replenish the water, carried on and secured the Coupe des Dames by seconds.

Paddy Hopkirk and Henry Liddon leading the works Minis on the way to scrutineering prior to the 1965 Coupe des Alpes. Pauline Mayman's car (DJB 93B) is behind, followed by AJB 33B of Makinen and Easter.

Aaltonen and Ambrose were not so lucky, finishing 14th, after a policeman sent them in the wrong direction immediately after a time control – Tony only noticed this after 10 kilometres. They made the next control with 67 seconds delay, despite driving flat out, and 'lost' their cup. Rauno lost the chance of a silver cup, awarded for all drivers who finish three times running without losing penalty points. By way of consolation he scored sufficient points to stay in the leading group for the Rally World Championship.

For the Polish Rally at the end of July, Aaltonen and Ambrose took over CRX 89B, Hopkirk's winning car from the Circuit of Ireland. They won convincingly. Paddy Hopkirk was the only BMC team member to contest the minor Nordrhein-Westfalen Rally. The organization proved to be abysmal and arranged so that only locals had a chance to lead. Hopkirk was clear on every special test and was furious when the organizers placed him sixth, giving first to a local Opel Rekord driver. He swore never to compete in that event again.

For Aaltonen the last two events of 1965 were of the utmost importance as he had to win if he wanted to be European rally champion: three cars were entered for the Three Countries event, Munich, Vienna and Budapest. Aaltonen/Ambrose (number 72) won overall and their class while Tony Fall and Brian Crellin were second in the class, driving a car that had been handled by Aaltonen as long ago as September 1964 in the Tour de France. The third Mini CRX 90B was written off by Halliwell in an accident; it was sold to Paul Easter later that year.

The regulations of the Three Countries Rally specified that no service points were to be set up. So Stuart Turner engaged a number of private drivers to follow the works drivers and provide service if needed. Aaltonen's service was assured by no less a person than Paul Easter, who followed Rauno with a car on cross-country tyres, to enable these to be fitted when the works car had to negotiate rough roads. Easter and Liddon carried almost 100 litres of petrol, tools and luggage for all four people in their Mini and still kept up with the competitors. After winning this event, which was run by Rauno's friend René Trautmann, all eyes turned to England where the traditional RAC Rally ended the season.

If Aaltonen became rally champion for 1965 the new Hydrolastic suspension, developed jointly with Dunlop, would have fully proved itself. The competition department had hesitated before adopting this interconnected system for the rally cars, because it was feared that the connecting pipes might be damaged in the rough and tumble of rallying. Also it had not been clear how the suspension could be tuned for different road conditions. Thus it was not until 1965 that the suspension – fitted to the Austin/Morris 1100 since 1962 – was accepted for the works cars. Rally use proved that the fluid, a mixture of water, frost and rust inhibitors, would function reliably in all temperatures and the connecting pipes to the individual suspension spheres would also remain tight.

Even at BMC the betting on the RAC Rally gave no clear guide – would it be Rauno Aaltonen with the Mini or Timo Makinen with the big Healey? Since they ran in different

Chasing overall victory in the 1966 Monte: Easter and Makinen apparently even have time to smile at the photographers, but there were no smiles later when they were disqualified due to wrong light bulbs.

classes nothing stood in the way of a possible championship as far as Aaltonen was concerned. So the prospect was for a truly fascinating duel of the year: the very quick Finns would soon discover whether front engine/rear drive was inferior to front engine/front wheel drive. Rauno was backed by another Finn, Jorma Lusnius, as well as Hopkirk, Fall and Kallström. At first Timo pulled out a long lead with the big Healey, but floundered in snowy Yorkshire. Rauno took the lead for a short time, but Timo's car was manhandled through a difficult few yards by spectators and he managed to catch Aaltonen again. A fascinating duel between the two Finns was decided in Wales, deep in snow. Rauno with the light front-wheel drive car managed to 'swim' the Mini through. A British car won the European Championship for the first time, a victory made possible by Aaltonen and Ambrose, who scored five of the eight victories that fell to BMC works teams. Thus ended one of the most successful and difficult rally seasons.

Changing regulations, and changing times

The 1966 season brought BMC its greatest triumphs, its biggest defeats and its severest trials: when Turner left BMC at the end of 1966 he could look back on 18 major rallies, and the season's results made a fine

farewell gift, coinciding with the marriage between BMC and Jaguar at the end of the year. Yet perhaps he would have done things differently had he known what awaited him at the first event, the Monte Carlo Rally. Four cars were entered: Makinen/Easter had a 1275 Cooper S GRX 555D, start number 2; Aaltonen/Ambrose drove GRX 55D; Hopkirk/Liddon had GRX 5D with start number 230; Baxter/Scott had GRX 195 with start number 87. The arrival of the works representatives was greeted frostily – the first, Wilson McComb, was asked by an elderly official whether they had arranged for the presence of mechanics in the parc fermé in case of protests at the end of the event. This question alone, prior to any other greeting, made it clear that the French had no intention of letting the Monte Carlo Rally fall to foreigners. The press also claimed that everything was not right at BMC, no way had they built the stipulated 5000 Cooper Ss in one year as required by Appendix J. In fact 5047 vehicles were built, but that did not count, because one could also read that if these really conformed to Group One they could not win the rally! If nevertheless BMC did win then it could always be proved that these vehicles did not conform to Group One..... As the French say: 'C'est le ton qui fait la musique'. When Stuart Turner went out to dine with friends in Monaco, the restaurant manager remarked

Championship clinched with a victory in the RAC Rally, Rauno Aaltonen and Tony Ambrose waste liquid on their Cooper S.

the mountains. 160 competitors started in Chambéry and the stage over the Col de Fontbelle was cancelled due to too much snow. Three of the special stages had little snow, which favoured the Porsche 911s and the Lotus Cortinas. Makinen was fastest on the other two and on the Granier five and a half minutes faster than in the 1965 snow storm. The pass was not even closed to ordinary traffic and Paul had to get officials out of a café to have his road book stamped. The new section decimated the field to 35 competitors, led by Makinen with 122 points, Aaltonen immediately behind him and Hopkirk a little further back. That evening in Monte Carlo no-one wanted to believe that the Minis had been quickest over two special stages. It was widely assumed that the BMC works drivers had covered the timed sections with specially tuned vehicles, which had lurked somewhere in the Alps in a truck and were indistinguishable from the other cars. No-one was able to prove this, and the organizers started to look for other irregularities.

The real story was entirely different: Stuart Turner was the first manager in rally history to send out recce vehicles, whose crews compiled notes on road conditions which were then entered in the co-drivers' road book. The advantages were obvious. For example, the run-in to the Mont Ventoux began with thick snow but before they started Turner was able to tell his drivers that apart from two bends the road was dry. As a result, summer tyres were chosen from the 572 tyres they had brought along. All the others put their faith in spikes – wrong decision.

Finally the tough final course through the Alpes Maritimes had to be tackled. There were three special tests on the Col di Turini, two on Mont Couillole and one on the Moulinet pass. During the 'night of the long knives' Porsches led three times, Minis twice and a Lotus Cortina was fastest only once. Yet the Minis could always be found in second, third or fourth places; and so in the final ranking Aaltonen was clearly in the lead, followed by Makinen; Günther Klass's Porsche was in third place and Paddy Hopkirk led the next Porsche by a second in fourth position. BMC had therefore won the Monte in 1964, '65 and '66 – in 1966 taking first, second and third place.

But the euphoria was misplaced. Even before the 'night of the long knives' the headlamps of all cars had been cursorily tested by making them switch from main beam to dip against a board and noting the result. No further details were given. Now the Minis were really put through the mill. It was a matter of course for the drivers not to go to bed despite being on the go for 16 hours in the final test, but to follow through the wearying eight hours of the technical inspection. The cars were stripped and every possible component weighed and measured. The officials used two ordinary bathroom scales. Naturally the engines' cubic capacity was measured, the suspension checked and even tyres taken off the rims and weighed. The alternator output was measured, although the method employed was more than dubious. Whenever the testers gleefully announced that they had found differences from the homologation papers, the BMC mechanics could show that they had taken the wrong measurements. At first the stroke was queried as too long; the BMC people noticed that the officials' data sheets referred to the 850cc engine, not the 1275cc unit. Then they found that the track on Hopkirk's car was 3.5mm too wide. The commission announced this first

when the bill was being settled: 'I'm really sorry that you won't win this year. Things will be arranged so that Citroën will walk away with victory'.

On top of this, the International Sports Authority had sent out regulation changes so late that many teams could not meet them. Some paragraphs were ambiguous and while some manufacturers tried to equip cars according to regulations, Volvo and Saab, who had participated in the Monte for years, withdrew their entries for the event. Nothing daunted, Turner entered his Minis, and, accompanied by Henry Taylor, Ford's competition boss, flew to Paris and the FIA to clarify many small points. Both returned to England certain that they could now prepare their cars to meet the regulations. Turner said later that there was no discussion concerning the type of lighting, because there were no questions on either side. BMC was sure of its facts.

The final changes in the regulations reached Abingdon when Paddy Hopkirk was already en route to Warsaw. Aaltonen/Ambrose started from Athens and Makinen/Easter from Lisbon. Everyone was in good spirits, although they sensed there might be problems. The widespread range of starting points meant some 2175 miles/3500km of motoring to Monte Carlo, to be undertaken in the production car seats. Despite Paul Easter's accident in Grenoble on his debut drive, Makinen entrusted the main road section to his co-driver. With a supply of port, sardines and white bread, he usually stretched out on a foam bed, the co-driver's seat being stowed temporarily behind the driver. This time there was no snow and the trip from Lisbon to Avignon passed off pleasantly.

For 1966, the Monte Rally used a 900 mile/1500km *Parcours Commune*, containing 6 separate timed stages in

It became routine to tip a Mini on its side for service or instant repairs. Hopkirk (in the foreground) and Crellin steady their car as it comes to rest on a cushion of spare tyres in the 1967 Acropolis.

This picture went round the world: on the Thousand Lakes rally Makinen's car ran too hot. Before one stage he unshipped the auxiliary lamps and fixed the bonnet as a temporary measure to the lamp brackets. After a characteristic 'yump' the bonnet flew up and Makinen had to continue the special test in this way – the public were delighted, the engine remained cool and Makinen only lost 19 seconds to the fastest competitor. He won the Thousand Lakes for the third time.

to the press – the British were hit in the eye in the afternoon by the headline 'A victory for truth', when it had already been established that such a variation was quite usual after 2800 miles/4500km of tough driving: the Minis had dropped on their suspension. Lifting the car corrected the track width. In the end the biased officials were only left with the dubious argument that the car's lighting system did not comply with French laws, although they were acceptable under the Appendix J regulations. The pretext was that the fog lights had been used as dipped beams as the headlights contained single filament halogen bulbs. The Mini-Coopers provisionally placed 1-2-3 (Makinen-Aaltonen-Hopkirk) were disqualified, and so was Roger Clark's Lotus-Cortina, provisionally fourth. Voila! Citroën had 'won'.

But the 'winning' driver, Pauli Toivanen, never drove for Citroën again, published photographs of Citroën mechanics changing the headlights on his DS21 were ignored, and BMC and Ford appeals against the disqualifications were turned down – by the French-biased body that had approved the lights before the rally!

Some of the French Press insisted that the British had always cheated – could anyone guarantee that a rally Mini had anything in common with a Mini bought from a dealer?

Yet the publicity for BMC was enormous and the sales figures leapt upwards, while Citroën benefited little from its 'triumph'.

The French specialist journal, *L'Equipe*, took a matter-of-fact view: it borrowed Paddy's rally car GRX 5D and ran back-to-back tests with a Mini Cooper 1275S from a dealer. Timo Makinen alternated with its editor Alain Bertaud, driving both cars at La Turbie with results that amazed everyone: the series-production Cooper was faster every time!

There were other moments in 1966. For Makinen and Aaltonen, the Swedish Rally was anything but a pleasure drive. Timo, in the lead, dropped out with a broken drive shaft. Rauno smashed his radiator against a rock and had to drop out with overheating. Things were no better in Italy: Paddy Hopkirk got best times early in the rally but then his Group 2 Mini also fell back into the middle of the field due to overheating. Tony Fall was not even admitted to the special tests because he carried paper filters for the air cleaner in the car. The Italians seemed also to be infected by anti-British fever: Vic Elford and his Lotus Cortina were disqualified because they counted one extra tooth on a gear-wheel than shown in the homologation sheet, which contained a printing error. It was a black year, but it spurred the team on. In Ireland local hero Hopkirk provided an extra setback: he reduced GRX 55D to scrap in a special stage.

Following Tony Fall's overall victory in Ireland, there was a major success in the Tulip Rally: Aaltonen won, followed by Makinen in 9th position. Together with private entrant Robert Freeborough they also took the marque cup. Only two cars were entered for the Austrian Alpine Rally, which Hopkirk won convincingly. Tony Fall hit a wood pile and bent the subframe and the steering beyond repair.

Preparation for the Acropolis had been really thorough: no question of collecting bits of car as in the previous year. The route proved to be so tough that Citroën decided not to participate. Of the 105 starters, two favourites stood out: the Lotus Cortinas of Elford, Clark and Söderström, and the Minis of Hopkirk, Makinen and Aaltonen.

The lead kept changing and so did team fortunes. First Timo hit a rock and tore off a suspension link, then Elford's gearbox stripped its gears. Aaltonen overheated and it was left to Hopkirk to battle with the two remaining Fords. The pleasure of winning only lasted until four minutes before the expiry of protest time: the rally officials penalized Paddy for arriving prematurely at a control point and for service within a control zone. Despite this the Mini held third place and the team left Greece with mixed feelings. Tony Fall then won the Scottish after a prolonged battle with Elford and the Saab 96 of Larsson. From Scotland the scene shifted to the Geneva Rally, where Tony Fall finished second in the overall classification in the Group 1 Mini, while Hopkirk dropped out with gearbox problems.

The London event followed and Fall led until he passed the wrong control and retired with technical problems. In the Prague Rally the team gained first, third and fourth and the team cup. Fall and Makinen were first

The scrutineers in action at Monte Carlo in 1966, desperately seeking a reason to disqualify the Mini Coopers, and at last finding a highly questionable one in the lights.

and second in Poland in August. The penultimate high spot of the 1966 season, the Thousand Lakes, became the battle ground for the rival northerners. Makinen, Aaltonen and Lusenius chose co-drivers with local knowledge and Timo won his favourite rally ahead of Aaltonen.

Rauno preferred the Alpine that followed and finished third behind the Porsche of Günther Klass and Roger Clark's Cortina.

This third place was remarkable as the Mini suddenly lost all electrics during the special test in Cannes. Co-driver Liddon did what he could and cobbled up a repair, but the pair missed their Alpine cup by 20 seconds.

BMC won the Munich-Vienna-Budapest event again, as in 1965; this time Makinen drove to an overall victory. Tony Fall had to retire due to technical defects.

For the RAC Rally in November BMC set up a battle force of seven cars, one driven by Grand Prix driver Graham Hill. He had the car that had won in Poland, while Fall kept his Alpine one. But hopes remained unfulfilled. In a dramatic rally, Bengt Söderström kept a Cortina in front. As soon as Ford heard about Hill's drive they entered Jim Clark. History does not relate how Hill got on with the Mini: he had no training and seemed glad to retire in the Lake District with gearbox trouble, while Clark's rally ended in a minor accident.

Although Makinen put up some quickest times and did lead, he was still unlucky, having to stop on the Yorkshire moors with an overheated engine, thus burying his last chance in the championship. Paddy Hopkirk, who had been among the front runners driving that season, could not maintain the lead he took over. He took a wrong turning at a crossroads, reversed, and stripped the 'box when accelerating again. Now it was Kallström's turn, and like his Swedish compatriot Söderström he headed the event in a British car. Eventually he at least saved the day for BMC by winning the class.

The 1966 season had not lived up to the expectations of the BMC bosses. They cut the competition department budget and Turner almost had to beg for money – a commodity by now in short supply within BMC. Stuart Turner must have realized that the future for the competition department was not promising and he handed over to Peter Browning, leaving after six years of effort.

Peter Browning takes over

Turner's successor was sought from inside BMC and Peter Browning, who had acquired experience in many rallies under Turner, was offered the job. Browning tried to turn down the job of competitions manager, perhaps feeling that he could not live up to Turner's record. But he was talked into taking it, and it was agreed that he and Turner would cope with the 1967 Monte Carlo jointly,

▲ In comparison with today's competition departments, the world-beating Mini Cooper then had only a smallish workshop in the MG plant.

▶ Before the 1966 Monte: Paul Easter, Henry Liddon and Tony Ambrose on the roof, with Aaltonen, Makinen and Hopkirk cheerful on the bonnet.

because preparations had already progressed quite far. Beyond that another 15 events were entered in his diary.

It has always been said that the 1967 season was not as successful as the 1966 one. But six outright wins, nine class victories and many good places in the most important rallies prove otherwise. As far as drivers were concerned most things remained as they had been; but for the Monte the Lampinen/Wood pairing was added to the line up. From the start the 1967 event was a snow rally yet again. While Aaltonen, Fall and Lampinen had dry roads for the run to Monte Carlo, Paddy Hopkirk had chosen the Athens start, hoping for good weather – but Yugoslavia provided really exceptional snow conditions. Yet the remarkable Mini 'roadability' in deep snow enabled him to arrive in Monte Carlo on time.

In 1966 the team had taken a selection of 572 tyres, but in 1967 regulations were different, permitting only a choice of tyres per car for the special stages. Each Mini had a robust roofrack to carry four alternative tyres.

Again the team 'ice-spies' proved their worth. Just before the start they reconnoitered the run so as to inform the

service crews of the exact tyre choice required. After the first mountain section, from Monaco to Chambéry and back, the Mini of Hopkirk was in second place behind Elford's Porsche 911S, followed closely by the excellently placed Timo and Rauno. Most importantly they were ahead of the Lancia Fulvia of Leo Cella and Ove Andersson.

The road conditions in this Monte caused the little 1275 Coopers great difficulties, for between sections of ice and snow there were long sections of dry roads which favoured the other competitors. Aaltonen managed nevertheless to keep 12 seconds ahead of Ove Andersson's Lancia, whilst Hopkirk settled in sixth place. On the other hand Timo Makinen hit a rock which dropped right in front of his car and destroyed the Mini's front, including the starter, distributor and oil cooler. Repairs set them back but finally Makinen and Easter by a great effort managed 41st place in the overall classification. On top of all this the weather took a hand in the result. Henry Liddon, co-driving the winning car with Rauno Aaltonen, recalled later:'It was the start of one of the special sections over the Col di Turini and I believe someone had had an accident on the section. Anyway, the start was delayed. The whole field waited patiently at the start when it began to snow more and more heavily. All tyres had already been fitted and fortunately we had decided on "Weathermasters"; no-one was allowed to change anything on the cars any more. The snowfall meant that we would have to cope with fresh snow on the Turini and Vic Elford in the Porsche was the only one to attack it before us. This is the moment when a man drives above himself and produces wonders. This is a peak in life and I have only experienced such moments once or twice, magnificent moments. After starting the decisive section of the 1967 Monte with a two hour delay, we felt we must win.'

The result is well known: Aaltonen/Liddon won after a dramatic struggle with Elford and also won their class. Hopkirk/Crellin maintained sixth place and on the final results list Tony Fall managed tenth, while Lampinen continued the Minis' good run and finished in fifteenth position. The results of the 1967 Monte showed that the organizers had learned lessons and were not about to repeat the previous year's manipulations. The red and white Minis gained their victory and enabled Stuart Turner to celebrate a win on his last outing with the Mini Cooper he had helped make so famous. The drivers could not have given him a better farewell present!

The Swedish Rally had seen the retirement of all the Mini entries in 1965 and 1966 and so it was hardly an auspicious first event for Browning. Two cars were entered in 1967, and yet again they were dogged by bad luck. Timo Makinen was let down by a lack of brakes. Aaltonen, with Liddon as co-driver, was lying in third place behind the Lotus Cortina of Bengt Söderström and the Saab 96 of Simo Lampinen when he ran into a snowdrift and somersaulted end-over-end several times. Luckily the car landed on its wheels and was still drivable. Badly shaken, Rauno and Henry restarted only to find that the rear window had been smashed and all their possessions, tools and spares were strewn over several hundred metres. But their lead over their closest competitor was so great that they managed to collect

This 'yump' made the rally yearbooks and calendars. Although the 1967 RAC Rally was cancelled, Makinen drove a special section for the TV cameras and gave the press an unrivalled photo opportunity. The car is the new fuel-injection Cooper S specially built for the British event.

everything and stow it in the car again without losing their place. At the finish the car's interior was not only very cold but full of exhaust fumes, and a tough time was had by the crew. But they managed to finish the Swedish Rally, a first for a Mini in that event and in third position to boot. Aaltonen and Makinen were glad not to have to start on the Rallye dei Fiori in San Remo the following weekend.

A San Remo 'fiddle'

One of the best Mini works team stories concerns the 1967 San Remo event of 1967. Paddy Hopkirk led Jean Piot in a Renault 8 Gordini until the penultimate control in Badalucco, high up in the mountains above San Remo and the end of the last special stage. About a kilometre before this control, placed at the beginning of a winding downhill run towards San Remo, a drive shaft universal joint broke – the run seemed over and Jean Piot sailed by. Paddy knew that from now it was nearly all downhill and found a tractor to tow him to the top. From there he rolled, engine running, down to the service point where Doug Watts and Peter Browning were waiting to service the car for the last time. They did have another joint in the car but changing it would have meant losing second place. Somehow the final control had to be reached. Paddy's eye fell on the 4 litre Princess R – and he proposed, in all seriousness, to have his car pushed to the finishing line! No sooner said than done. The service crew jumped into the Princess, Doug at the wheel, and shunted the Mini forward. Luckily it was

downhill and the bumper bars were nearly at the same level. To complicate things, half-way down the hill towards the finish there was a time control, fortunately on a steep section. Paddy, wildly 'changing down', screeched to a halt, and co-driver Ron Crelling held the papers out to be stamped with much gesticulation; meanwhile the Princess braked sharply and distracted attention. After the papers had been stamped, Paddy simulated a poor start with a badly 'slipping clutch' and slowly rolled away. The Princess had overtaken him and was waiting beyond the next curve to 'connect' with Paddy again. The closer they came to San Remo, the more spectators and photographers made it difficult to keep up the deception.

But the best was saved for the end: fortunately a tunnel gave a chance for a last push, 'up to 30-40mph' recalls Peter Browning, and the impetus carried Hopkirk into the parc fermé, where he had to stop among journalists. When it came to parking the Mini, he just had to fake engine failure....

Everyone was worried that this form of 'propulsion' had been obvious to all but, wonder of wonders, no-one mentioned this curious chase to the finish by the two British cars. Only John Davenport, the British co-pilot of Ove Andersson's Lancia, wondered how a universal joint could be changed so quickly.

Mini in Africa

After the freezing Swedish Rally Aaltonen and Henry Liddon were off to the heat of Africa with the winning car from the 1966 Munich-Vienna-Budapest event.

This was the team's first entry in the East Africa Safari. Aaltonen made his special requirements known to the competition department, to meet the anticipated tough road conditions. Thus the department created a very special Mini, with Hydrolastic suspension which could be pumped up for extra clearance on bad roads, by means of a rear mounted pump. Aaltonen also insisted on 'snorkels' for the inlet and exhaust for deep water work. Strong handles were fixed to the bodywork, for manhandling the car out of mudholes and other

Engine room of the 1966/67 works 1275S Cooper rally car, showing the controversial carburettors.

situations. The car was also fitted with top-mounted wipers that could also be worked manually.

The Mini had been proved in snow, but it was poorly equipped for the 1967 Safari mud-battle. After very heavy monsoon rain, this event entered history as the wettest East Africa Safari ever. Despite thorough preparation, one of the many mudholes put paid to the Mini's engine, which had taken in mud and water.

There was some consolation for Peter Browning when Paddy Hopkirk won the Circuit of Ireland outright with the 1966 Monte Carlo car, thus scoring a fifth victory on the Emerald Isle. He left England to conquer new fields, entering the Three Hour Race at Sebring. GRX 309D, the winning car in Poland in 1966, was uprated with a 1275cc engine for this circuit race.

The Tulip Rally featured spring-like weather and dry roads, conditions that did not favour the Minis. Not surprisingly the favourite was the team's old rival – Vic Elford's 230bhp Porsche. He seized the opportunity and avenged himself for the Monte, narrowly winning from Makinen and Aaltonen. Those who claimed that the Mini could not take a lot of punishment learnt to change their views. Timo broke a piston after half the special stages and could only carry on with constant oil replenishment and plug changes. Aaltonen who followed him could tell by the smell of burnt oil that his team mate was still in the running and on the heels of the Porsche. Backed up by a good finish

by the Belgian private entrant Vernaeve the team recorded its only team prize of 1967.

The Mini's fifth attempt on the Acropolis followed retirements on a regular basis in the first three years. Hopkirk was third in 1966, and the battling Irishman was determined to win in 1967. The main rivals were the Lancia Fulvias and the Lotus Cortinas with the famous twin-cam engine.

Aaltonen, who had retired due to engine trouble the previous year, was not lucky in 1967. Shortly after the start Rauno suffered a frontal collision with a Volkswagen belonging to a local who met him head on on a closed road. This wrote off the Mini. All those in the accident had to be hospitalized, Rauno with slight

In 1968 the Mini rally team had no fewer than 731 Dunlop tyres at its disposal – from circuit tyres to the spiked winter tyres at the bottom of this pile.

Paddy Hopkirk outside the Ministry of Transport in 1968....

concussion and Henry Liddon with bruises. Thanks to the roll-over bar and full harness belts, the two drivers got away with only slight injuries. Rauno and Henry left hospital to join Hopkirk's victory celebration – he had realized his dream and managed to win the Acropolis after a dramatic battle. His co-driver Ron Crellin almost knew his pace notes by heart and they so divided their tasks that they could hold off Andersson and Söderström without overstraining the Mini. Finally, Paddy had to prove that he could park backwards, as in the old days,

The Prague rally was a tarmac event which did not favour the Mini, so Aaltonen and Liddon had to work hard to win outright in July 1966.

and slalom round the pylons, before a final timed hill climb. He started that with a lead of three seconds, and had to overtake a car which had started four minutes before him.

The Greek organizers had also thought up a spectacular final race on a small circuit; it did not influence the final rally results, as long as the competitors managed to cross the finish line. The three leading cars collided and Paddy's Mini lost its radiator water, and soon the engine overheated. But as always Paddy showed himself a cool customer, and before the engine finally expired he declutched and rolled to a stop five metres before the finishing line. There he waited calmly until the race director unrolled the chequered flag to signal the end of the race. After the first competitors had taken the flag Paddy turned the starter key and crossed the line on the starter motor.

The 1967 season had provided the works team with good results so far. After a second place in the Scottish Rally the flag was flown in the Geneva Rally. For this Browning entered the two 1275S Coopers that had been run in the Tulip Rally and taken first and second places there. By way of thanks for his support in the Dutch event, the works offered Vernaeve the team car LRX 827E while Tony Fall drove LRX 829E (start number 79). The organizers

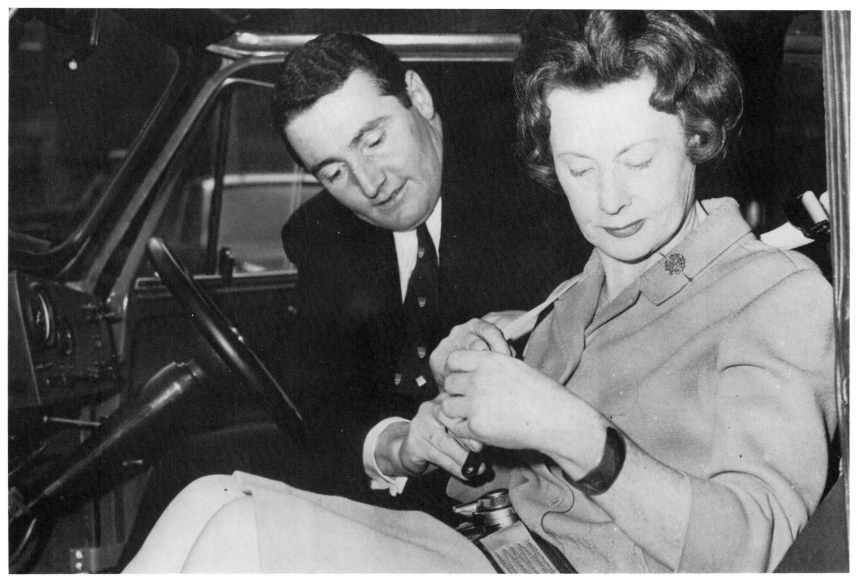

....shows the then Minister of Transport, Barbara Castle, the advantages of safety belts.

caused confusion to start with by running the traditional rally only for groups 1 and 3, while groups 2, 4, 5 and 6 were entered for a newly created event called 'Critérium de Crans-sur-Sierre'. That is why at the end there were two winners – the Rally itself went to Vic Elford's Porsche 911S, while the Minis were first and second in the Critérium.

The RAC ends the rally season. In 1966 Paddy Hopkirk was partnered for the first time by Ron Crellin, in a pairing destined for much success the following year.

Only Tony Fall started in the London Rally, in the car GRX 5D, which had won the 1966 Monte and in 1967 the Circuit of Ireland. This time it did not want to play and Tony Fall retired.

The Danube event foundered for lack of a piece of paper, as the civil servants in Prague affirmed that Aaltonen, a Finn, needed a visa for Czechoslovakia. When it was discovered that he could obtain this document without problem at the frontier, Aaltonen started. Unfortunately he did not get far as the frontier officials were not prepared to provide the required document. Thus the entry for the Danube Rally finished almost before it began.

Timo Makinen had an adventure in the Thousand Lakes Rally back home in Finland; he struggled hard for first place against his Finnish compatriot Simo Lampinen in a Saab before winning for the third time. When his engine temperature rose to critical heights Timo removed the upper auxiliary lamps whose attachments also locked the bonnet and drove on with the bonnet slightly open. On one of the jumps ('yumps' in 'Finnglish') the rubber fasteners holding the bonnet down parted and it blew open, obscuring the windscreen. For more than ten kilometres spectators saw Mini number 29 being driven wherever possible with the righthand door open and Makinen straining to see the road. He only lost 19 seconds on this special stage and won the Thousand Lakes on his home ground for the third time.

There were only two more major events in 1967 as the RAC

Henry Kallstrom showed his ability in the 1966 RAC Rally by taking second place overall, plus a class victory, ahead of Aaltonen/Liddon.

Rally was cancelled due to an outbreak of foot-and-mouth disease.

The 1967 Alpine saw four Minis entered. This sizeable battle line seemed a wise precaution, for the cars were in for a rough time, and in terms of speed had little chance against the Porsches and the very quick Alpine A110s. Tony Fall made a mistake, his Mini left the road and was badly damaged. Fall and his co-driver were not hurt but the car was not rebuilt until the 1968 season. Aaltonen gave up with gearbox damage. Makinen had to contend with overheating in the ski resort of Alpe d'Huez but managed to hold third place behind the two blue cars from Dieppe. On the second stage Timo moved up to second place due to the retirement of Jean Vinatier's Alpine – but he too had to retire with engine and brake problems.

Once again Ron Crellin's excellent preparation paid dividends for Paddy Hopkirk in the last remaining 1275S Cooper. Just as in the Acropolis, the two men were a good team and they conserved their forces. When thick fog descended Crellin, having learnt his pace notes by heart, was able to predict each corner exactly. Towards the end Paddy actually overtook Larrousse in the pea-souper. The Alpine seemed not to like the Alps and went on strike before the fast return run to Marseilles. The last of the competition was out of the running, and Hopkirk and Crellin reached Marseilles with a three-minute lead over the Alfa GTAs of Consten and Gamet.

It would have been too easy to leave the Coupe des Alpes cars in Marseilles, for the last event on the programme was the Corsica Rally. In those days drivers had to take the cars back to the works – or take the train! But the cars were badly knocked-about and needed an overhaul.

For the island event, Hopkirk and Crellin used GRX 5D, which had given up on the London but had battled into second place in the 84 hour event at the Nürburgring. Aaltonen and Liddon insisted on JBL 172D, with which they had such a fiery adventure in the previous year's Acropolis. If the two had had advance warning that the Corsican venture would founder on some minor components, the trip to this last of the year's events would perhaps not have taken place. The cars had run only a few kilometres when screeching fanbelts announced that drive from crankshaft pulley to the dynamo and water pump was no longer certain. The engines would not withstand the high temperatures resulting from insufficient cooling and gave up with blown cylinder-head gaskets. The mechanics could not understand the problem because they had changed the fanbelts as usual and tested their tension. Re-checking showed that faulty belt material was to blame, hardly a consolation for such an expensive and wasted effort.

1968 – the last year in main-line rallies

Modern rally cars today do not remain competitive six years running, even if their homologation lasts. Today's machines are transported on trailers and only have to last for the event, then they are transported home again. In the 1960s it was customary for competitors and vehicles to motor to the start and, if at all possible, return under their own steam. At the end of the decade the BLMC works team cars were some of the last to enter the events in traditional fashion. The Porsches and the increasingly powerful Alpines, on the other hand, were the first rally cars to arrive on transporters.

At a service point in the 1968 Monte Carlo Rally Aaltonen's car, lying in third position, gets a swift check-over. The Makinen/Easter car (Number 7 in the background) had lower priority because they had dropped far back.

Once again considerable investment was the order of the day for the 1968 season: no-one would have guessed that it was to be a dry season as far as rankings were concerned. The truth was that other competitors were managing to

Timo Makinen's driving style endeared him to all Mini fans. The 1967 Monte winning car became world famous even among children when Corgi came out with a model of it.

which mainly concerned the question whether the carburettors had been modified – forbidden by the regulations – or not. BLMC stated that it was a case of prototype carburettors made from original equipment components and, welded and riveted at the essential places, subsequently fitted to the homologated inlet manifold. The organizers' suggestion that they could be swopped for the old SUs was unacceptable to Peter Browning, because they could not be procured within a day. While another meeting was in progress, a false rumour was spread to the effect that Paddy Hopkirk was in the parc fermé changing his carburettors. To the BLMC people it was quite obvious that Paddy neither had carburettors for changing nor would attempt this without prior consultation; it was then proposed to interrupt the meeting for a visit to the parc fermé to find out whether Paddy really was working on the car. Rejecting this proposal, the officials decided to allow the Minis to start, but it was pointed out that in case of protest by another competitor, the decision would go against the cars. Peter Browning was certain that the other teams would agree with him and that no protest was to be expected.

Apart from a few minor incidents, the rally was undramatic. The Minis' results when considered against power-to-weight ratio were better than impressive: the

put more and more power onto the road. The programme included participation in 11 events, but in fact only 8 were undertaken.

The usual round began again with the Monte Carlo Rally, which brought almost as many problems as the 'protest' event of 1966. For the first time the Minis had twin-choke Weber carburettors, which had been further developed for this use at Abingdon following Timo Makinen's suggestions. Roughly speaking, the Webers were sawn through the centre, both left halves then being fitted together and mounted on the Group 2 manifold. The improved breathing increased power by some 7bhp but other teams had power advantages of up to 70bhp. Peter Browning was uncertain whether the new carburettors could be homologated and sent precise descriptions and photos to the Féderation Internationale d'Automobile (FIA) in Paris. No objections were received, so details of the improvements were passed on to the motoring press.

After the teams arrived in Monte Carlo there was a sudden technical inspection and the scrutineers advised the authorities that they were unable to accept the carburettors. This time the organizers proceeded with care to avoid any claims of favouritism. After a conference they informed Peter Browning that they were certain that the other competitors would protest if BLMC were to use the 'do-it-yourself' carburettors. After this decision a tug-of-war began between Peter Browning and the authorities

Even in January there can be sunshine. Tony Fall was tenth overall in the 1967 Monte Carlo Rally.

Alpines weighed 760kg, including crew, and had 120bhp, while the comparable Porsche figures were 1150kg and 180bhp. The Minis had to move a whole kilo per bhp more, because they weighed 800kg and had 110bhp engines. The situation was even worse for the Lancia Fulvias, where 950 kilos were propelled by 120bhp.

The final results seemed to prove these calculations: Alpines led but dropped out after being pitilessly pursued by Elford's Porsche. The quick Minis followed, under attack by Lancia. On the Col de la Couillole stage, a Lancia Fulvia with the 1.3 litre engine was even faster than the Minis, by one second. On the final stage, Aaltonen put up a time of 104 min 54 sec, Fall 104.55 and Hopkirk 105.16 – only 21 seconds behind. This final Monaco-Monaco stage was covered by the best Lancia man, Leo Cella, in 105.29 but he could not match Jean Vinatier's 103.28 in an Alpine. Fastest of all was Vic Elford in a works Porsche in 101.2, faster than his team-mate Pauli Toivonen by 27 seconds.

Larrousse dropped out after sliding off sheet ice, so the final results saw Porsches first and second, Elford/Stone leading Toivonen/Tiukkanen. Third place went to Aaltonen/Liddon, then Fall/Wood and Hopkirk/Crellin, then the first Lancia. Whilst there were no protests from the other competitors, the organizers were again very pernickety. Apart from the obligatory technical check after the event, all three Minis were submitted to further tests. Peter Browning kept cool with difficulty when he found out that the official in charge of scrutineering had been the fly in the ointment in 1966. When the scrutineers went to lunch after four hours of work, they did not even bother to look at the winning Porsches. However they were unable to discover anything to contravene the regulations in the Minis.

With hindsight critics say that 1968 was not a successful year for the works team. But a closer look will show that the Minis simply could not cope in performance terms with the drastically increased power of their competitors; it thus became necessary to overstress the vehicles at every event so that the cars eventually failed. The pushrod engines were tuned beyond their limits and were competitive in long-distance events only if the more powerful contestants fell out. Belgian driver Vernaeve managed third place overall and a class win in the 1968 Tulip Rally; Rauno Aaltonen again finished fifth and won his class. Class victories also fell to the Minis in the Scottish and TAP Rallies. The latter went to Paddy Hopkirk in October 1968, driving LBL 606D, which had first been used by Tony Fall for the 1967 Monte. As the 1968 season finished so ended the BMC team's great period in international rallying, although private Mini Cooper entrants continued successfully for many years.

There were echoes of the great days in 1969, when Hopkirk was runner-up in the Circuit of Ireland and took a class win in the Tour de France. Names from the past and promising newcomers were fleetingly associated with Minis in national rallies – John Sprinzel, for example, and Roger Clark.

Minis were around in rallies at this level, as well as in club events and well down the field in main-line rallies, through the 1970s and 1980s. In the 1970s they seemed to be increasingly used on road events rather than on forest tracks – an aversion to rough conditions rather at odds with the numbers so prominent in trials and in rallycross, a particularly rough form of motor sport, albeit events were very short by rally standards.

For a while there was a works effort in rallycross, until TV and spectator interest declined as the cars became more and more 'special' – or less and less like road cars, or circuit and rally cars. There was a recovery in the late 1970s, when there was some independent Mini development (such as a 16-valve version of the A series engine, which made little impact, a dozen years before the Warrior twin-cam version was reported). Minis, with that oddly stiff jumping action, remained very much part of the rallycross scene until inevitably numbers began to tail off.

During the 1980s historic rallies became firmly established, and Mini Coopers proved to be very popular entries. The first event of any standing, the RAC Golden Jubilee Rally in 1982, most appropriately fell to Paddy Hopkirk in the S that Makinen had driven to win the 1965 Monte Carlo Rally.

The Pirelli Classic Marathon was first run in 1988, and despite some misgivings soon became firmly established. Its route from London to Cortina d'Ampezzo included roads that had been used in Alpine Rallies and Marathons de la Route (Liége-Sofia-Liége) in the golden days of rallying. There were eight Mini Coopers in the 1989 event, and the third Marathon saw Paddy Hopkirk and Alec Poole win in a 'Paddy Hopkirk Mini Cooper S Works Replica'.

This was one of the very small number built by Poole and Simon Wheeler on the basis of pre-1966 1275 S cars, so this blend of old car restoration and rally preparation is authentic, and honestly eligible for FIA historic events.

Appropriately, Hopkirk flagged off the 1991 Pirelli starters, and the winning car was again a Poole replica of a works Mini Cooper S. At the end of a rather controversial event, Ronnie McCartney and Beattie Crawford just beat the Coulter/Howcroft Mini Cooper S. The Mini still thrives, in one of its elements...

Happy trio at a garage in 1967 – Paddy Hopkirk, mechanic Dudley Pike and Tony Fall before the Rallye dei Fiori on the Italian Riviera.

Just like the old days – Hopkirk and Poole with winners' laurels atop their Mini Cooper S in Cortina after the 1990 Pirelli Marathon. Their car is flanked by the MGBs placed second (Gammons and Easter, on the right) and third (Moss and Shields, left).

Not much room in the engine compartment of the fuel injection car. The inlet is in front, necessitating the repositioning of the alternator, top right, above the engine because its place is taken by the injector pump. The coil is also moved to a new spot, on the left above the brake servo.

John Cooper turned up at a works car reunion in Switzerland in 1984. The car was second in the Scottish Rally of 1968, was then sold to Richard Lawrence and later went to Switzerland.

Makinen and Easter in the 1967 Tulip Rally, when they won their class and finished second overall.

Despite handles, a high exhaust, powerful lamps and a carefully sealed engine, this Mini of Aaltonen/Liddon could not cope with East African conditions during the 1967 Safari.

MINI on the Circuit

Nobody directly concerned with the Mini was greatly inspired by its competitions potential, at least before the launch – after all, the combination of 34bhp and front-wheel drive did not seem to promise much – but once news of its phenomenal road holding began to circulate British tuning specialists looked hard at it. John Cooper looked at it, too, from a Grand Prix team base and racing car construction plant that was little bigger than some tuning establishments. His enthusiasm and his growing friendship with Alec Issigonis were to lead to the Mini Cooper, and a glorious international competitions record for the little box. He saw it as a circuit car rather than a rally car, and to a degree its racing promise had been demonstrated before the end of 1959.

That was at a grass roots level, where Mini racing still thrived in the 1990s. For 25 years from 1966 the Mini Se7en Challenge series – the idiosyncratic presentation of the original Austin name for the car was retained throughout – stipulated the 850cc engine, then in 1991 the 1-litre unit was specified. That apart the regulations were virtually unchanged, encouraging home preparation and making for ideal low-cost *ab initio* saloon car racing. The parallel Mini Miglia Challenge, a series that was all of three years younger, allowed greater freedom in engine and suspension tuning, together with wider wheels and slick tyres. The real point about these series, running from the 1960s on into the 1990s, was that they were in no way historic and brought quite exceptional continuity to one-model racing. Late in 1959 a venerable and much respected saloon car competitor, Doc Shepherd, drove a Mini to a class win in a minor event at Snetterton. The car was prepared by ace tuner Don Moore, and the engine had a Weslake cylinder head. Other independent entrants followed this example, and through 1960-61 the Mini became popular with club racers, to the extent that in 1961 the first one-model all-Mini race was run.

Eventually Issigonis' objections to tuned versions of his little brainchild were overcome, in part as he was persuaded that a series-built high-performance variant was feasible.

The 1-litre Cooper was attractive to club racers, and the performance demonstrated by Cooper's 55bhp engine gave it wider appeal. Soon there was an 80bhp Formula Junior derived power unit, useful for the 1-litre saloon class that thrived in Europe. Nevertheless, the first significant international race victory did not come until 1962, when Bill Blydenstein headed a Cooper team 1-2 in the 1-litre Coupe de Bruxelles, where the pair clearly beat a field largely made up of oddities such as two-stroke DKWs.

Cooper ran a works team, with cars in the colours of the F1 team (green with white longitudinal stripes) driven by Sir John Whitmore, John Love, John Handley, John Fitzpatrick and John Rhodes – one has to assume coincidence in the forenames! There were others, Warwick Banks, for example, while for long-distance events the rally

Cooper driver McKenzie has his mirrors full of Graham Hill's Jaguar at Brands Hatch in August 1962.

Rally drivers going round and round – Rauno Aaltonen in the 1275S he shared with John Aley in the 1963 Motor Six Hours at Brands Hatch and (below) Paddy Hopkirk in the car he shared with Whitmore, taking sixth place overall in the same race.

Why use brakes? Tyre-smoking cornering, practised by top-flight Mini drivers in the second half of the 1960s, was guaranteed to please crowds. Here Gordon Spice leads Rhodes and Handley at Brands Hatch early in 1967.

team drivers were sometimes given a circuit outing. There were other successful teams, among them the Alexander and Broadspeed outfits, and BMC helped by homologating a wide range of Special Tuning components.

Towards the end of the 1960s BMC went through a belt-tightening phase, and also took the works-associated team 'in house', to become a works team running cars in the red and white rally team colours. Coopers then ran an independent team of yellow and black cars. In 1969 Alec

Poole took the British championship with a 1-litre car prepared by Jim Whitehouse of Arden. His engine was reputed to give up to 112bhp, while the A series engine bored out to 1293cc for the 1300cc class, and with eight-port heads and fuel injection, produced some 140bhp. However, in terms of points scoring, competition between Mini drivers in the 1300cc class was often self-defeating...

For a while the Mini Coopers seemed to be eclipsed, and the spectacle of tyre-smoking cornering by exponents such

FIVE SPEEDS

The market for new performance components for Minis has been active for more than a quarter of a century and in the 1990s still justifies new design and development work. Jack Knight five-speed gearboxes are an example: the first was introduced in 1967, and was only modestly successful; the second was announced in 1991.

The main problem with the 1967 'box was the space limitation, for the original transmission casing was used. This was modified for the 1991 gearbox, which allowed larger gears to be accommodated, with adequate bearings (the gears in the earlier box were slightly narrower, and room was found for the fifth gear by the deletion of the synchromesh). In both cases straight-cut gears were used, and the 1967 version was noisy...

The basic ratios (alternatives were available for first and fifth) of the two 'boxes were:

	1967	**1991**
1st	2.53:1	2.315:1
2nd	1.60:1	1.568:1
3rd	1.24:1	1.195:1
4th	1:1	1:1
5th	0.865:1	0.915:1

Jack Knight also produced associated limited slip differentials, a ZF type in the 1960s and the GKN Salisbury unit under licence in 1991.

The Jack Knight Development five-speed gearbox introduced in 1991.

More tyre-smoking – a Cooper pair, Rhodes leading Steve Neal, at Brands Hatch in 1968.

as John Rhodes was sadly missed by spectators. In the 1970s the circuit future for the Mini seemed to lie in the one-model series and from 1973 in British special saloon racing, a curious category for odd hybrids and Group 2 cars left over from the preceding championship seasons (the British championship was run for Group 1 cars from that year). The Mini was also prominent in autocross and rallycross through to the second half of the decade.

That was the time when British Leyland (as BMC had by then become) started to promote the Mini in racing again, introducing a 1275GT championship, in which a fair degree of tuning was allowed, and 'adopting' the Mini Se7en and Mini Challenge series.

Then in 1977 the Mini became prominent in British main-line saloon car racing again, especially as Richard Longman started to campaign a Group 1 1275GT in 1977. In Patrick Motors cars he won the RAC Saloon Car Championship in 1978-79 through his successes in the 1300cc class (each class scored equal points in the overall championship). A higher weight limit told against the 1275GT in 1980; Longman moved to Ford, and Jon Mowatt's third in class was the best showing for a 1275GT.

That year the 1275GT championship gave way to the Metro Challenge, but the two older series were to continue into the 1990s, usually healthily. In more open championships Mini drivers enjoyed some success in the 1980s although their numbers slowly dwindled. But in round terms that was happening more than a quarter of a century after the little cars' first circuit appearances, and they had been enormously popular and enormously successful.

Rhodes again, with a Group 5 Mini Cooper S that has obviously been in contact with another car at Silverstone in 1969. This version had a fuel-injection engine and outwardly was distinguished by its wider wheels.

Mini Cooper
Principal racing championships

Year	Driver	Title
1961	Sir John Whitmore	British, 1000cc and overall
1962	John Love	British, 1000cc and overall
1963	Rob Slotemaker	European, 1300cc
1964	Warwick Banks	British, 1000cc
		European, 1000cc and overall
1965	John Rhodes	British, 1300cc
	Warwick Banks	British, 1000cc
1966	John Rhodes	British, 1300cc
1967	John Rhodes	British, 1300cc
1968	Gordon Spice	British, 1000cc
	John Handley	European, 1000cc Division 1
	John Rhodes	European, 1300cc Division 2
1969	Alex Poole	British, 1000cc and overall
1972	Jonathan Buncombe	British, 1300cc

The Mini was a competitive circuit car right from the start. This appears to be a near-standard car.

A works Mini Cooper S in full flight at Silverstone in 1965.

In historic touring car racing the Mini is still flying the flag around the world. At this 1987 meeting in Germany a 1964 Cooper S is showing its heels to an NSU Prinz.

Mini Mayfair with optional cast-alloy wheels.

Mini 1000 MkIII.

The Mini 1000 engine is an unsurpassed example of compact construction. Left, the clutch and its control and the starter. Where engine and clutch assembly join, the oil pressure pipe to the gauge can be seen below the ignition coil. The heater valve is next to the valve-cover but without its pipe. The new inlet manifold with pre-heating is seen on the inlet side; there is a plastic radiator fan and an alternator.

MINI Specials

The Mini has inspired enthusiasts and small firms to produce conversions or original sporting cars using Mini components. From the many interesting designs the most important are described in alphabetical order, with their features. This is necessarily historic for very few of these specialist constructors survived very long.

AB1 - Sandy Fraser's Three Wheeler

British Road Fund tax laws favour three-wheelers and designs like the Morgan three-wheeler and the Bond became well known. In 1971 designer Sandy Fraser set up a small company with a view to constructing a three-wheeler based on Mini parts. In its basic layout this recalled the Morgan. At first he called it the AB1 and used a complete Mini front subframe together with the Cooper twin-carburettor engine. The protruding front wheels were covered by small mudguards and access to the

Sandy Fraser's AB1.

Sandy Fraser's Grand Prix.

cockpit was by climbing over the low sides. Similar to the Morgan, exhaust pipes ran hip-high to the left and right toward the rear. A small hood and a screen provided some

weather protection. The body was of laminated wood with a teak frame and covered in sheet metal. It cost £275 as a do-it-yourself kit. This three-wheeler with its single rear wheel was further developed into the Spider model and after Fraser moved his workshop to Marlborough in Wiltshire he developed the Spider as the Grand Prix. But only nine of these had been built by 1987.

Biota

Racing driver John Houghton was one of many who looked to Mini components as a basis for a sports car. One problem for designers intending to fit the Mini

Biota.

engine/drive unit at the front is its height, which makes it difficult to achieve a low, smooth line. Houghton's design for the body of the Biota got over this by incorporating a big air scoop in the bonnet that neatly accommodated the engine's height. The car had a tubular frame and the glassfibre body had crisp, attractive lines. There were no doors, so getting in or out demanded a degree of youthful agility, but prospective buyers of Biotas would not have been put off by that. There was a prominent roll-over bar behind the seats, and the little Biota offered fresh air motoring in the Lotus Seven spirit.

Houghton showed the car in 1969 as a kit car and it was well received, but there were teething problems and only 30 had been built by the time the project closed down in 1976. The Biota was intended as a road car, but one – admittedly specially prepared – gave its two drivers first and third overall in a British hill climb championship in 1972.

Buckle

Australian Bill Buckle built some 30 Mini GT fastbacks in 1966-67, with a fibreglass roof which curved down rather weakly into the tail to merge with the normal boot line. The front seats were lowered to improve head room, which perhaps made for a rather odd driving position as apparently the height and rake of the steering column were not changed.

Butterfield Musketeer.

Butterfield

The British have been keen on plastic bodywork since the 1950s, and the accumulated expertise has meant that small runs of hand-built small cars have been feasible. In 1962, Butterfield showed a small coupé at the London Racing Car Show. It was 40 inches high with the legend 'Musketeer 1000' inscribed on its side. The plastic body hid a Mini 850 or Cooper engine, the bonnet opened *à la* E-type Jaguar, and while the front portion of the side windows was fixed, the rear panel was hinged. This appealing coupé cost between £850 and £892. Perhaps the Musketeer was before its time – no more than three vehicles were actually built.

Camber

The work of George Holmes and Derek Bishop, who ran Heron Plastics, the Camber GT was built in Bishop's

Camber GT.

garage in Camber Sands, Sussex. It had a glassfibre body with steel reinforcement in the roof, and a tubular chassis on which Mini subframes were mounted front and rear. The car was well built but fell foul of a law requiring a minimum height for the headlights. The Camber GTs were too low, and only six were made. Derek Bishop dropped out of the project and George Holmes took it on on his own, renaming the car the Maya GT, and revising the nose so that the headlights met the legal requirements. Unfortunately he was killed in a road accident in the winter of 1968, by which time only six Maya GTs had been sold,

Davrian.

and production ceased.

Davrian

One of the Mini's main competitors on the British market was a car made by the Rootes Group, the Hillman Imp, launched in 1963. It was slightly larger than the Mini but it was rear-engined (with an advanced 875cc ohc power unit) and gained a reputation for unreliability and odd handling. It came three years after the Mini, and that handicap was too great.

The small Davrian company in Wales used the Imp as the basis of a plastics-bodied rear-engined coupé, but when Imp production ceased Davrian had to consider other mechanical components. So they looked at the Mini and integrated its two subframes into their glass-fibre monocoque. The engine remained at the rear, requiring air intakes in front of the rear axle. With only 38bhp but weighing only just over 1000lb, this little sports car could reach a surprising 95mph with the headlamps retracted. With more powerful engines a top speed of 120mph was possible. Later the Dyfed-based company used Ford Escort engines to keep up its power image. Davrian still make kit cars.

Davenport

It is amazing how much work enthusiasts are prepared to invest in an idea which will never result in series production. Such an enthusiast was the sports car driver Derek Davenport, who at first welded together an elaborate multi-tube frame which gave a very long wheelbase and was meant to take both Mini subframes. But the 1300 GT engine finished up in the car's centre, requiring considerable modifications to the rear drive and suspension. His 1975 sports car used the external door hinges of the earlier Minis, but he placed the big fuel tank above the front axle and attached the long glassfibre front wings to the original Mini wings. Thus the

Davenport 1300 GT.

headlamps were high enough to comply with road traffic act regulations. Despite so many clever details the Davenport appeared very much 'hand-knitted' and remained a one-off.

Deep Sanderson

Many designers were frusatrated by the high bodywork of the Mini and endeavoured to achieve a lower profile in their own creations. The Mini engine's height stood in the way of these ideas, although it saved in overall length.

Deep Sanderson 301.

Chris Lawrence, another racing driver, was one of the first to place the engine at the rear to improve the car's aerodynamics. He also completely rehashed the Mini and on his own initiative built a true central-tube chassis, strengthened by a box section frame. A gifted technician, he could not come to terms with the series-model subframes and devised a special suspension system with trailing arms connected to the springing at their pivot points. Lawrence worked hard in the three years after the announcement of the Mini, for his car was raceworthy for

the 1962 season. Front and rear opened fully from the passenger compartment outward and completely exposed the mechanicals in the manner of the later Lamborghini Miura. 301 was the type number of the first Deep Sanderson. It had a Vauxhall Victor windscreen, was roofless and, as in the Ferrari 'Breadvan', there was a small rear window in the rear panel.

After a successful 1962 racing season there was a demand for replicas, and the 'production' 301 appeared at the London Racing Car Show in 1963. This had an attractive coupé body, somewhere between an Abarth and a Porsche 356, with a nicely shaped nose section. The rear still opened as a whole (the engine cover plus its carpet covering rose up, totally exposing the engine) and this necessitated a roof joint at the B post which Lawrence never managed to make quite watertight – customers who bought the 301 coupé in kit form complained about that. From technical points of view the 301 was successful: with the 997cc Cooper engine it managed 108mph. It was only 57in wide and only 36in high. Ground clearance was only 5.5in and the owner had to pray for smooth roads. But despite thoughtful design and an attractive appearance production never reached appreciable numbers, only 14 being sold.

Fletcher GT.

Fletcher

In 1967 Norman Fletcher bought the manufacturing rights to the Ogle Mini, which had first seen the light of day in 1962. His company in Walsall gave the car a new and not very attractive nose. It was a failure - selling all of four cars hardly made the company's fortune....
(see also Ogle Mini)

GTM

The British somehow lose their proverbial reserve in their approach to sporting vehicles and this must be the reason why the Cox GTM caused such a furore at the 1967 Racing Car Show. In fact it was just one of many small coupés which were theoretically though not always in practice available. Bernard Cox, however, had constructed a real mid-engined sports car in his garage

GTM was mid-engined.

excluding the wooden parts and those taken from the Mini. He added a set of plans and recommended that in case of difficulties the local joiner should be consulted. In Towns' opinion, an average cabinet maker should be able to construct the monocoque of the Hustler from plywood. The whole vehicle should then cost some £1200, depending on the cost of the donor Mini. Inside room in the Hustler was considerably better than in the Mini and with a large glass area. One entered the vehicle through two sliding glass doors; a partially glazed roof could also be opened. The Hustler had side mounted seats in the back, reached via a large rear door, and one then sat inside as on a veranda. The wooden version was also available in three axle form, or as a small van. An improved version from 1983 was made partially in glass fibre plastic, topping a multi-tube frame.

in Cheshire, a car that could be competitive and be used as a commuting vehicle to the office. A considerable number were sold.

His recipe was based on the experience that write-off Minis are still useful, if all the usable components are salvaged for re-use with a plastic body. The steel box section chassis drawn by Cox only accepted the Mini subframes after elaborate modifications. The main problem was the position of the power unit.

This plastic body could be altered in certain ways. Early examples had an oil cooler in the front, but the later GTMs had a spoiler instead of an air intake.

The most recent version, much improved in detail, is called the GTM Rossa and is available in roadster and coupé forms.

Hustler

William Towns' Minissima design of 1973 created considerable interest, and when it became obvious that it would not be put into production, he started out on a project of his own. Towns considered the high degree of enthusiasm for DIY and added one of the most attractive designs to the existing range of British wooden cars. From 1979 he offered (for only £900) all the necessary kit, but

Jimini

The makers of the Yak were not the only ones to recognize the need for a follow-up to the Moke, but after they closed down in 1973 two years passed before another Moke-clone to appeared. Its creators took even more trouble and made the Jimini entirely of steel. Once again the car used the ingenious Issigonis subframes - they were bolted under the rigid body platform and voilà it was finished! Thanks to the subframes the wheelbase could be freely altered due to the absence of a fixed link such as a propshaft between front and rear. One might say that whilst the two subframes are commercially available even a bathtub could be motorized!

Hustler by William Towns.

Jimini.

Issigonis was largely responsible for BMC 9X, a possible successor to the Mini. It was wider and had more headroom but there was no extra luggage space and this 1968 prototype again had sliding windows. Issigonis ultimately came out against it, because the individuality of the Mini would have been lost. Advanced power units were proposed for 9X.

The front quarter view of ADO 70 as built by Michelotti to Longbridge designs was very attractive and, as early as 1970, it had a T-roof with removable halves. The excellent use of internal space of the Mini was sacrificed – this was a two-seater.

A look inside ADO 70 with one roof panel removed shows instruments from the 1275GT, a new wheel, good bucket seats and a developed but sober dash. The workmanship of this hand-built prototype was exceptionally good, but that also brought a weight penalty.

The rear view was perhaps not so satisfactory, but there was excellent luggage space. The roof halves could be stowed behind the seats.

But back to the Jimini: soon a dispute arose between its designers. After 12 vehicles had been built, they decided on a rethink at the end of 1975. Then half way through 1976 the Jimini reappeared with a sloping bonnet, rectangular headlamps and a new front panel incorporating a wider grille. Production ran into hundreds and shortened and six-wheel versions were available.

Landar

Landar was known to motorcycle fans before Mini racing cars had been heard of. This Birmingham company

Landar R6 sports-racing car.

manufactured motorcycle parts for sporting riders and supplied the two-wheel industry with original equipment in the days when Birmingham was the home of prestigious motorcycle marques. However, the industry slipped into deep trouble and new ways to gain publicity through sporting involvement had to be found by the brothers Radnall.

While working for the Radnalls engineers Williams and Pritchard discovered the Mini's potential as an inexpensive racing machine, especially because – surprise, surprise – the subframes made individual designs much easier. Their dreams gave birth to the fastest Mini-based racing car ever. The first Model – R6 – had a box section chassis with a glass-fibre body and was victorious under the name of Landar (Radnall backwards, leaving off one L). The first test runs showed that the 35in high sports-racing car could reach 132mph with the 997cc engine. This was only the beginning: equipped with the best Cooper engines and the tallest gearing 150mph was possible and 0-60mph took some seven seconds! It cost then £900, without the rear mounted engine and transmission components; 40 cars were sold. Drivers like Frank Aston competed in the 1000, 1100 and 1300cc classes both on circuits and hill climbs.

The R7 which followed had the 1300cc engine fitted in the rear of a multi-tube frame. It was inclined forward by 20

degrees and the R7 won the SCCA 1300cc Sports Car Championship in the USA. Most of the R7s went to the States (in 1970 some 10 cars were built). But Landar Components lost money on each R7 and were glad to sell the moulds and rights of the R7 to Canada in 1972.

Magenta

The wave of buggies on VW chassis in the seventies inspired a lot of people to construct their own vehicles. Most buggies had one-piece bodies which only needed the attachment of the power unit and equipment. It was therefore hardly surprising that the buggy movement looked to the Mini. Lightspeed Panels in Lealholm near Whitby was a company specializing in trim panels for caravans, interiors and show stands. They modified an 1100cc buggy which was already in production to accept Mini and Austin/Morris 1100 components and offered this vehicle in 1980 as the Magenta. The engine stayed in front together with its subframe, a tubular frame covered by a plastic body extended to the rear with the suspension arms of the Mini, controlled by spring-damper units. The wheelbase was longer than the Mini's.

Externally, as usual on buggies, there were no doors, two seats only, and a space behind these from which a roll-over bar seemed to sprout. The spare was on the tail.

Marcos

Marcos cars in Bradford-on-Avon came to work in different ways for BMC, for apart from building the Mini-Marcos in their own right, they had a development contract from BMC - but more about this later. This Wiltshire-based sports car builder showed the Mini-Marcos in the spring of 1965. It was sold as a kit of parts which contained the following: an unpainted plastic body with all the necessary mountings and fittings, a separate chassis, and windows with rubbers. The engine and subframe were obviously not included in the price of £199 as used Minis were available everywhere.

At the 1966 Racing Car Show the egg-shaped Mini-Marcos, an ultra-low plastic sports car, seemed quixotic, but promised exhilarating performance. The two-door coupé – there was no hatch – could be had to choice with the 850, 997 Cooper or Cooper S engine. The chassis was quite able to cope although the original Mini wheelbase was retained.

Soon after the Mini-Marcos' debut, the car was made available in three stages of completion: the most expensive at £380 came fully painted, glazed and with the wiring loom in place. But only the fourth version was really successful: the Mk IV had an opening hatch, was slightly longer, and was now built at D&H Fiberglass in Oldham and no longer by Marcos themselves.

As early as 1966 the Mini-Marcos fitted with the 1275cc Cooper S engine gained world renown when Marnat and Ballot-Lena ran one at Le Mans with the competition number 50. They managed a surprising 15th (and last) place overall with an average speed of 89.69mph, a sensational figure for a 1300cc car with a maximum speed of 123mph! In Britain the Mini-Marcos put up excellent performances in circuit racing and hill climbs through to the seventies. Later, Ford BDA engines were fitted and there were further modifications.

In 1970 Jem Marsh, whose name coupled with Costin to make 'Marcos' and who jointly owned the company, came up with an ambitious plan to extend the range beyond the successful Marcos sports car, which survived into the 1990s. The futuristic two-plus-two luxury coupé was called Mantis and was a flop, aggravated by a dubious racing venture with a similar looking machine; Marcos went into liquidation and had to shut down. Jem Marsh managed to save at least the Mini-Marcos, with the help of enthusiast Rob Walker. Manufacturing finished up in a small plant at Westbury, where the smell of laminates and resins continued until 1975 when D&H Fiberglass bought the rights and production tools of the Mk IV, which sold 700 units between 1972 and 1975.

Harold Dermott, the new owner, planned to build on this success, simplified the production process and started with a basic price of £645 for the kit. But the flowering of the Mini-Marcos was past - its somewhat strange shape did not ring too many bells and ex-Jaguar engineer Dermott began thinking about a successor, asking the industrial designer Richard Oakes to re-work the concept, while Oakes was still a student at the Royal College of Art.

Dermott took the ex-Le Mans car to Paris to exhibit it and hopefully sell it. Unknown 'enthusiasts' forestalled him and stole the car – it was never to be seen again. Harold Dermott flew back home to start preparing for the Midas which will be dealt with in the next section.

The relationship between Jem Marsh and BMC brought up a further project at the end of the sixties which should be mentioned here. The great success of the Mini encouraged Leonard Lord and the BMC management to press forward with the idea of a 'world car', for countries which did not possess steelworks or competent pressing facilities, but on the other hand offered good marketing prospects for a small car like the Mini.

Towards this end BMC made two attempts to develop a plastic-bodied Mini for production.

The first project, developed at Longbridge, produced an

Mini-Marcos goes racing.

D&H Mini-Marcos gained a hatchback.

Autocars Marcos, intended for production in Israel.

113

all-plastics Mini body, without the characteristic guttering, on a ladder frame. It was intended for production in Chile.

The second project, in 1969, involved Marcos, and the intended manufacturer was Autocars of Haifa in Israel. Marsh used a monocoque plastic structure without the ladder frame, but with the familiar subframes and a long-nosed front, similar to the Clubman's. As far as possible original production parts were used, including the windscreen, and with Innocenti window frames in the doors he achieved a Mini-like appearance. Five plastic Minis saw the light of day in Bradford-on-Avon, four estates with long side windows and a fastback with a hatch. But during crash testing development came to an end, for BMC sold its shares in Autocars due to the uncertain situation in the Near East. Marcos then sold the fastback to an American battery concern which re-built it for electric propulsion. Where the other four cars are is not clear, although two are said to be in the hands of British Mini enthusiasts.

Midas

Although the kit-car market in the UK was in one of its periodic troughs D&H Fiberglass went to work on the Mini-Marcos after having acquired all the rights from Jem Marsh. As mentioned, with Richard Oakes' styling assistance a new sports coupé was developed from the Mini-Marcos, having almost identical dimensions. Its smoother surfaces were easier to mould and cheaper to produce. Harold Dermott, the ex-Jaguar engineer, undertook development; he now turned his back completely on the old Marcos, having 'lost' the Le Mans car in Paris. Mechanically only slight changes were made, such as a wider track, and the Oakes design was adapted into a monocoque. The Midas now had a practical rear hatch and small rear seats, the bumper bars were raised to the height of other cars and, sub-frames apart, the Midas was now rustproof. Due to the tall engine unit only a small, steeply raked windscreen could be used.

Originally the Midas was equipped with the Mini 1000 engine, unless clients provided the good old 1300 Cooper S, when 100mph was on the cards. The Midas gained a formidable reputation for its road-holding, and in 1989 a most attractive open version appeared, the Gold Cabriolet,

Midas.

which like the Gold used Metro rather than Mini components. Then a factory fire brought production to a halt, and Dermott had to sell the assets of the under-capitalized company.

Mini-Jem

This little sports car shared its roots with the Midas but the Jem in this case was Jeremy ('Jem') Delmar-Morgan. The confusion is understandable, especially as the Dart project was a starting point for both cars, and Jem Marsh left that for Marcos. The Mini-Jem only debuted a year after the Mini-Marcos and, in its production period until 1975, changed ownership three times. When Fellpoint Ltd in Buckinghamshire gave up production, 250 units of the Mini-Jem had been produced – details apart, they were almost like brothers to the Mini-Marcos. The Mk II, listed 1969-75, had impressive performance potential with a maximum speed said to be 105mph.

Mini-Jem engine compartment.

Mini-Scamp

The Mini-Scamp is the rolling proof that a Moke can be designed without a curve template and can even become quite a sales success. The background of this angular design was the desire to provide even modestly-skilled DIY enthusiasts with a kit of parts they could build up. Robert Mandry, who fathered the Scamp, supplied a solid tubular frame, which his customers covered with much aluminium sheet. A hack-saw, ruler, nuts, bolts and a rivetting tool were the only tools needed to construct an estate, delivery van or pick-up – no matter whether the vehicle had four or six wheels – or an ultra-short chassis for city use. All this became possible by means of the Mini subframes, which accepted the tubular chassis.

After building more than 700 units a strengthened frame and a new body were introduced and the new, even more angular, box was called simply Mk II. The first examples of this 1978 horror even boasted extravagant gull-wing doors. These were, however, rejected by the clientele because the roof could not be opened whilst driving, nor could the screen be folded flat. Small car fans who enjoyed design seemingly issuing from the sketchbook of a primary school child could still buy the Mini-Scamp through the 1980s.

Mini-Scamp.

Mini-Scamp Mk II with gullwing doors.

Minissima

The best looking and smallest of all Minis shone out on the British Leyland stand and stole attention from other exhibitors at the 1973 Motor Show, in part because not much new was to be seen that year, except the AC3000, the Clan Crusader and the winning exhibit of a design competition. However, the newcomer was a concept car, never a production model.

This smallest of Mini derivatives was given the name of Minissima since a little vehicle called Minima had already appeared at the Paris Salon - it really was the right name for this William Towns design. He was then working for Aston Martin in Newport Pagnell, where his main job was designing the new, futuristic, wedge-shaped Lagonda based on the DBS V8. For the

William Towns' Minissima had a single rear door.

Minissima, Towns positioned the Mini subframes as close together as possible and devised a new seating arrangement: there was room to pass between the front seats and behind them, attached to the sides, was a seat on each side. Thus the Minissima had only one door, at the rear, so it was a relatively high town car. Towns argued for this solution since it avoided bulky side doors and made parking in narrow spaces possible. To leave room to pass between the front seats, the Minissima was fitted with an automatic gearbox, whose selector was on the sharply inclined dash. British Leyland used the car for two years for PR purposes, then it was decided not to proceed with series production due to a number of

Minissima interior with gear selector on right.

serious disadvantages: the front bumper was too high, the front end could not be fitted with commercially available headlamps, the power unit was so far forward that the licence plate would be fitted to the gearbox and even small collisions would cause major damage. On top of this, the public authorities would not permit a car without side doors. They used a reversed 'Isetta' argument, stating that in a rear collision no-one would be able to get out of this attractive town car. Yet the Minissima showed the way to the town car of the future and the model makers Corgi thought it worthwhile to reproduce it in ⅟₃₆ scale as their number 288 from 1975.

Nimrod

A Mini-based creation appeared in the spring of 1973 looking at first sight much like an amphibious machine and, with its enticing name, promising extra performance. At that time the name Nimrod was synonymous with the very latest technology, for a surveillance aircraft based on the old Comet IV was being designed, which seemed preferable to the USA-built AWACS.

The creator of this road Nimrod might have done his planning more thoroughly, for the doorless open car with its all-round bumper strip was not exempt from VAT. The front-engined car with its plastic bodywork only found five buyers; the moulds were sold, but it still awaits resurrection.

The short-lived Nimrod.

Nota Fang

The Nota Fang was almost a 'street racer', built by a Sydney company which produced Clubman sports cars on Lotus Seven lines. Its actual designation was Type 4, and apparently just over a hundred were built between 1971 and 1975.

The designer was Guy Buckingham, an expatriate from the UK. Fortunately the Mini was popular in Australia (it was built locally 1961-68) where it was very successful on the circuits in the 1960s. Guy took the front subframe, fitted it in the back and designed a very reasonable independent front suspension, not quite hidden under the pointed nose. Small mudguards turned with the

Nota Fang was built in Australia.

wheels and two tractor headlamps sat atop the shock absorbers. The Fang had a small, flat windscreen but no doors – one entered it as a formula car. It was quite fast, with a top speed up to 105mph, depending on the engine. Access to the engine was achieved by lifting the whole of the rear including the Targa bar, and air ingress was through intakes in front of the rear wheels. In the UK the Nota Fang came with the new Dunlop Denovo wheels and tyres, but its appearance told against it: no more than three vehicles were sold, complete save for engine/transmission and its subframe.

Ogle

Ogle is a name to be conjured with in British design, for it has been associated with underground trains, helicopters, interior design for all kinds of vehicles, office equipment and trucks, to name just a few. David Ogle founded the company at the end of the fifties in Letchworth and became successful as a design consultant to British industry. When the Mini came on the scene, Ogle decided to try to make the little vehicle into a sports car, without unduly impairing its

Ogle SX1000 was particularly well finished.

usefulness. The SX1000 shown in 1962 was a fully plastic-bodied coupé with the 997cc engine. It boasted a practical rear hatch and despite its sloping tail incorporated two small rear seats. The finish of the SX was of a high standard because Ogle had already had experience with glass-fibre reinforced resin on his Riley 1.5 litre-based car. The well-fitting doors had wind-up windows and the exhibition cars were trimmed in Connolly leather. Ogle hoped to sell the car particularly in the USA, where the increasingly stringent safety regulation did not apply due to exemptions for cars produced in small series. So his sales manager Andrew Hedges and racing driver Sir John Whitmore took off for a goodwill tour of the United States, but found no real market for the tiny car there. Whitmore himself got to like the Ogle to such a degree that he bought the demonstrator on his return and gave it to his wife.

The plastic body enclosed the entire Mini floor pan, reinforced by side members. Unfortunately the front end was rather long so that some of the Mini's compactness was lost. Yet British orders flowed in, so that in 1963 six SX1000s a week were made. In that autumn the real driving force behind the idea, David Ogle, died when he crashed in the prototype Ogle Lightweight GT, a variant of the SX1000. Soon production of the SX1000 came to an end, as the company was losing money on every one sold.

Seemingly, some 66 Mini GTs and SX1000s were built, whilst the 850 Mini GT was in the minority due to its maximum speed of only some 75mph. The cars, fully fuelled, weighed 590kg and 615kg and had a reputation for great reliability: some, such as the racing driver John Handley, used them until the end of the sixties. The Ogle Mini was certainly the most mature product among many – but that was not enough for success under new ownership and Fletcher, the boat and caravan manufacturer, was unable to bring the Ogle back to life.

Peel

This 2+2, built on the Isle of Man and using Mini components, was in the same category as the Ogle, Mini-Marcos and Midas. The Peel made its appearance at the London Racing Car Show in 1966 as the Viking Sport and could only be bought in kit form. The complete plastic body with original Mini windscreen, rear windows from the Fiat 600, and doors exactly like the Mini's, cost some £250 from Peel. The subframes, engine and so on had to be bought and restored by the customer separately. Yet this Mini coupé with its aerodynamic nose attracted some 25 customers before production ceased at the end of 1968.

Pellandini

This ambitious sports coupé appeared in Adelaide, Australia in the early 1970s, using Mini engines and mechanical elements in a sleek and low – and most unMini-like – body. Eight were built as gullwing coupés and one as a convertible before the project came to an end.

Ranger

On through the 1970s and 1980s small manufacturers still used the Mini as a basis for specials. Ranger in Southend also wanted to make use of the three-wheeler road tax concession and designed the Cub, which was delivered in one piece to the customer, who then fitted the engine and transmission on the Mini subframe. At the rear, a single trailing suspension arm from the Mini was attached to a

Ranger Cub three-wheeler towing rather a big caravan.

Ranger Cub four-wheeler was a pick-up.

Peel Viking Sport: note the standard Mini doors.

reinforced mounting. Modified steering, plus the fuel tank from the Mini, were added and the open Cub was ready to roll. In 1974 Ranger published a press photo showing the Cub towing a caravan - there was no mention of the spartan hood or the open luggage compartment. Nevertheless some 200 customers bought this strange three-wheeler.

In 1975 Ranger turned to a four-wheeled pick-up. They simply used the usual subframes and attached a bath-shaped load platform to the open plastic body. The rest remained as before: there were no side windows or doors and people had to climb in over the cut-away sides. At the end of 1976 Ranger got into difficulties and only four four-wheel Cubs were sold.

Siva Mule.

Siva Buggy aped the VW style.

Siva

At Blandford Forum in Dorset designer Neville Trickett tried his hand with two creations, for quite different markets, which were shown to the public in 1970. He created a really chic beach buggy, a two seater with a roll-over bar that was very true to its name. A quick look might make one think of a VW buggy, particularly due to its 13 inch wheels. The massive roll-over bar with its bracing contributed considerably to stability. Under the curvaceous skin lurked the Mini subframes, whose rear ends protruded nonchalantly into the air just in front of the wheels. A small tonneau covered the trough-like luggage compartment, driver and passenger were cosseted in sports seats, there was a Motolita steering wheel and the bonnet was graced by Citroën 2CV headlamps. People with sporting ambitions could have an oil cooler and Wolfrace light alloy wheels fitted with Dunlop SP tyres, but these were obviously not included in the £195 which the kit cost. The purchasers also had to buy the two Ford Transit rear-view mirrors separately, but this seemed no deterrent for the 100 or so customers who went for the Buggy.

Alongside the Siva Buggy, a small all-terrain vehicle of 'corrugated sheet' design appeared in 1970. Recalling the departed Mini-Moke, Siva called it the Mule, thinking that Moke fans would enthusiastically buy it. The Mule was quite well built: its 12in low-profile wheels carried a plastic

body with rectangular wheel apertures which were partially corrugated for added strength. The flat windscreen could be completely removed and there was a wide roll-over bar. Between the bar and the windscreen canvas doors could be clipped on when the weather turned bad; these together with a hood were meant to give adequate protection.

The driver had a single windscreen wiper which covered a maximum of half the screen and good Cibié headlamps provided light. While it was well thought out and of acceptable quality the Mule did not make it: only some 12 buyers paid the basic price of £195 for one.

Status and Minipower

On his departure from Lotus designer Brian Luff optimistically turned to the design of an open roadster in the spirit of the Lotus Seven, but avoiding the shortcomings of the current Series 4 Seven. Luff had a lot of talent, having also helped to design the Clan Crusader. In his design office he had created the 'Workmate' bench which Black and Decker later produced. The Minipower was quite costly: a plastic body covered a multi-tube frame, and there was all round double wishbone suspension. The engine sat amidships behind the seats. Small mudguards turned with the wheels and the sporting layout ensured impressive performance. Luff provided Formula 1 roadholding and unequalled driving feel. Nevertheless the time for such puritanical roadsters was past, for the Minipower suffered the same fate as the Nota Fang: after some 15 vehicles had been built production ceased because there was no demand. Luff opined: 'pity really - the Minipower was too good - pearls before the swine!'

Status Minipower.

Status 365.

His other businesses prospered however, and he had time to work on a new project. The Minipower had been developed in his kitchen and after completion had to be taken out through the window - but for the Status there was a workshop. This was to be a wedge-shaped Mini for the family, but the devil must have looked over Luff's shoulder. Together with John Frayling, who had designed the latest Lotus Elite, he came up with a remarkably ugly body. To simplify construction, straight edged lines were chosen, and the windows were flat-glazed and clumsily shaped. The frog-like headlamps sat above the surrounding sharp edges of the bonnet, which opened in one piece. Despite the large glass area only a small slot opened when the windows were wound down, because a large quarter light in front and a door-handle at the rear inhibited the window-lift mechanism. The chassis was just as unconventional – a monocoque of plywood and fibreglass mat accepted the two subframes and was bonded to the orange-coloured body. When the first prototypes were built, the car's potential as the basis for various electric-powered vehicle projects was explored, as well as its potential as a city-car project, but from 1974 the Status 365 was on the market. Luff's sense of humour simply combined the type number with his confidence in its daily use, 365 days in the year. It would have been interesting to know who the 21 customers for the Status

365 were - they certainly were not getting a status symbol.... yet that had been Luff's idea for the company name: he was annoyed with all the poseurs who demanded a five-speed Lotus, although its four-speed gearbox harmonized much better with the engine. So he designed a gearlever knob that displayed an eight-speed gate and offered this accessory under the Status label with considerable success to all those who 'only' had a four-speed Lotus.

A little later he manufactured a nice 'Rolls-Royce' grille, exactly right for the Mini but called Status; after some 80 examples had been sold Rolls-Royce took action to end their sale. Luff has never revealed whether the Status 365 was meant as a joke.

Stimson

Barry Stimson is one of those designers who added variations to the Mini theme: he spent ten years developing projects and bringing them to fruition. He started with the Mini Bug of 1969/70; then came the Bug II from 1971 to 73, the Safari Six, shown in August 1971 and built until March 1973, the Stimson Mini Bug CS+II from 1976, and then the three-wheeled Scorcher, available until 1979.

Stimson claimed the title 'first buggy based on the Mini' for his 1969/70 Mini Bug; it was a real fun-mobile for leisure use. The £170 kit contained a plastic body, a chassis for mounting the Mini subframes, and, at the back, telescopic legs from the motorcyle world in place of the rubber suspension. The first model had wide, fat wheels that protruded from the body and a frameless plexiglass screen like a motor boat. A roll-over bar and smart sports seats enhanced the sporting appearance. The dashboard curved gently into the sides and contained only the round instrument from the 850 Mini - there was nothing else. To accommodate the radiator, the matt-black bonnet had a hump on the left. The actual cooling air intake was below the registration plate and below a belt-line which revealed the chassis to all and sundry. Stimson, barely thirty years old at the time, was rightly proud of his work and actually found 20 buyers for his fun-mobile - until the improved Bug II came on the market.

Stimson Bug.

Stimson Safari Six.

modifications consisted of rubber sleeving the ignition and a wire screen between the alternator and radiator. Below the flat front end hung a shovel-shaped spoiler, and the front axle carried wide Minilite wheels. The Scorcher boasted peculiar roadholding due to its single rear wheel and needed much driving practice; but that was secondary to becoming accustomed to the hand throttle and brake lever, rather like the vehicles used by the handicapped. Safety was conspicuous by its absence, and the driver slid about on his seesaw, only able to cling to the steering, which was not really intended for that purpose. Thirty enthusiasts must have liked the idea of combining riding a horse, driving a car and straddling a motor cycle, but whether any Scorchers remain is not known. What might Stimson's thoughts have been on seeing the 1985 'Machimoto' by Ital-Design, when they took up the idea of the Scorcher?

The 1971 model now had a proper screen with surround and wiper, the protrusion on the bonnet became significantly smaller, and below the 'beetle carapace' there was a combined spoiler-cum-bumper with seven big holes for cooling air. Apart from small design changes, visitors to the Racing Car Show in January 1971 noted a wide, plastic roll-over bar on the tail which simultaneously provided a frame for the rear screen and support for the lightweight hood. Some 160 orders flowed in over two years and even BL asked the designer for a test car. But he already had new ideas: from August 1971 he presented his Safari Six, rather like a customized Clubman but on six wheels. Back to the A post the car was based on the series-poroduction Clubman, including the windscreen, but with a different grille. From the A post all similarity ceased: the body sides rose up above the rear wheels and served as a sort of gunwale over which one had to climb. Four independent Mini trailing arms with very wide tyres held up the rear and carried the large load platform. Overall length was 138in, for one of the fat spares was hung at the back. There was no hood and only two seats, but a large tonneau cover was supplied. Obviously there were some lovers of big game hunting with exotic small cars: some twenty Stimson Safari Sixes disported themselves on British roads but production ceased in March 1973.

For three years Stimson picked up his profession as boat builder in Brighton again and tried to make good the losses on his vehicle production - then he caught the buggy fever once more. He showed the CS+II, based on the Bug II, in 1976. Stylistic changes mostly concerned the front section and interior details – all the body moulds could be used again. At the same time he developed his Scorcher - a fast three-wheeler that supposedly lived up to its name, but only provided him with grief. The rights of the CS+II had to be sold to Mini Motors of Rochdale, who built a few CS+IIs through to 1979.

But what about the Scorcher? It was simply too frightening for public traffic. One had to sit astride it like a motorbike, but instead of handlebars it had a wheel. The feet rested on wide running boards which formed part of the resin-reinforced glass-fibre body. The series-built 1000cc engine sat in front of a small plexiglass screen; the engine's only

Terrapin

Soon after the Mini became popular, clever amateur mechanics had a go at single-seater versions which might eventually compete in a one-type formula. There have been a number of attempts at Mini formula cars, for example the Terrapin, Fireball and Dastle. Northerner Allan Staniforth designed the sole successful monoposto, the Terrapin, for circuit racing and hill climbs. In so doing he had to solve many problems. First, new wishbone suspension for all wheels had to be devised to attach to a light space frame, then modified steering was required, and the front radiator was a long way away from the mid-mounted engine. A long run of water piping led from the nose to the engine behind the driver's seat, the expansion tank came from the top of another radiator, with its filler, and the additional oil cooler fitted into the roll-over bar. Fuel was kept in flank tanks. The Terrapin Monoposto managed a few 'succés d'estime' but never really succeeded due to lack of reliability.

TiCi-Mini

The shortest Mini conversion also had the shortest production run, although no less a person than Stirling Moss promoted it and, accompanied by Mini-girls, travelled far and wide to sell the open TiCi. Perhaps the people around its designer, Anthony Hill, overlooked the fact that it was not a good thing to use GAY in the licence plate - the connotation of the word was too suggestive. Be it as it may, production of this cheery rear-engined device ceased in 1973 after some 10 units had been built, some of which had a roof extending to the rear, but no doors.

Trimini

The British road tax system favours three wheelers and traditionally there have always been British buyers happy to take advantage of this concession, but some wanted vehicles that were more ingenious than Reliants or Bonds. Bond recognized this trend and built the orange-coloured Bug, which was even exported and made into a Corgi model. Auto Bodycraft in Staffordshire thought up an open Mini, with a central wheel at the rear, a complete Mk I front in plastic and a boat-shaped rear. For £400 the buyer

Terrapin Monoposto with polished alloy bodywork.

obtained a complete Mini subframe with an engine under the plastic bodywork and a coil sprung wheel at the rear. Between 1969 and 1973 25 purchasers considered that this conversion would suit them, and that concluded the case for the Trimini.

Unipower

Originally commissioned by racing driver Roy Pierpoint, the first car was built by Andrew Hedges with an aluminium body. The project was then bought by Tim Powell and when the car went into production in 1966 it had a fibreglass body. Initially it sold quite strongly for a car of its type (50 road cars and 5 competition versions in the first two years), then the project changed hands. The new company, Unipower Cars Ltd, did not prosper and folded in 1970 after making approximately fifteen cars.

Widely regarded as one of the two best Mini-based cars ever made (the other is the Midas), the Unipower GT had its engine/gearbox unit in the back of its space frame, just ahead of the rear axle line. Suspension was independent all round by coil springs, the gear lever was mounted on the right hand door sill, and the fibreglass body was bonded on to the frame to create a rigid structure which contributed

to the car's outstanding handling. Cooper versions of the Mini engine were used, the 998cc version propelling the GT to 100mph/160kmh, while 120mph/193kmh was obtainable when the 1275cc engine was fitted.

Yak

When Mini-Moke production was transferred to Australia in 1968, there were many disappointed Moke fans. The very original Moke shape, despite the inadequate weather protection, must have been the reason for the love affair between drivers and this spartan vehicle, and there were several attemps to revive the Moke. At the same time the sports car maker TVR was in difficulties and Bernard Williams and John Ward left. The two of them did just what they had done at TVR and designed a tubular chassis suitable for a plastic body. Yet this time it was not a sports car but a vehicle similar to a Moke, based of course on the mechanical components of the Mini. Even the front screen, electricals and most of the equipment came from it. Since Williams and Smith had only limited space, they sold their Yak only in kit form. To the end of production in 1973 some 150 die-hards had decided to buy this plastic 'donkey'. In 1991 the 'real' Moke returned.

Unipower GT, one of the best Mini-based cars.

The Yak, more ungainly than the Moke.

Innocenti MINI – The Italian Jobs

Innocenti, based in Milan made the Lambretta scooter in the 1950s and started manufacturing cars with a licence-built version of the Austin A40. An attractive Ghia-bodied version of the Austin-Healey Sprite followed, then BMC's 1100, and the Mini in 1965. The Mini proved successful in a Fiat-dominated category, as young Italians took up this lively small car enthusiastically. The Innocenti version's interior equipment was always more chic than its British sister, yet even in 1970, when the Mark III was already on the British market, the Italians had to make do with sliding windows, outside door hinges and the early radiator grille.

When the firm's founder Ferdinando Innocenti died in 1972, only the Mini 1000 with the 998cc engine, the Mini Matic with an AP automatic transmission, the Mini Cooper 1300 (local name for the 1275S) and the Estate T1000 were being produced. The 'luxury' version of the Mini 1000 was designated 1001, and was not that luxurious. The Mini Cooper 1300 was top of the range, fitted with the 1275cc engine from the GT. After Innocenti's death British Leyland bought the Italian company for £3 million and started to rationalize the model programme. For the British and other export markets, the fact that the licensing agreement with John Cooper was only signed in 1965 turned out to be an advantage later – the ten-year contract enabled BL to continue Cooper S production in Italy until the end of 1974, whereas this model was dropped from the British catalogues in July 1971. Quick-thinking importers could therefore ensure that at least Continental customers were still able to order a Cooper S, although the UK market was excluded.

The Mini 1001 had winding windows, and the quarter lights originally designed by chief stylist Haynes. Milan insisted upon its own distinctive grille, and also went its own way with the interior. The Mini Cooper 1300 had a sporting three-spoke steering wheel and a row of four small instruments, plus two large round ones. A water temperature gauge, ammeter and oil pressure gauge flanked a big rev counter (7500rpm) and a speedometer calibrated to 200kph, with a fuel gauge alongside. All instruments came from Veglia Borletti and were fitted into a moulded plastic panel, the whole incorporated below the screen where the old parcel shelf had been. The Italian Cooper had a black interior with attractive grey carpeting. The seats were in velour cloth with leatherette side panels; they were Italian made and seemed luxurious when compared to the British seats.

The Innocenti Mini 1001 had individual touches in details such as the grille, hubcaps, headlamp rims and side repeater flashers.

The de Luxe version Innocenti 1001 Automatic had cord-covered seats, a modern steering wheel, and a fully trimmed dash. A radio was fitted in the central console.

▶ A lhd export Mini Cooper of the 1970s with German equipment (in Italy the front flashers were white). While the dash is in poor quality plastic, the extensive array of instruments pleased enthusiasts.

These good-looking Minis were very popular, especially in Switzerland. The Italians kept faith with this body until the end of 1974, but they never took to the Clubman versions. They had their own body factory and, with British blessing, commissioned Nuccio Bertone to design a new shape early in 1973. At the beginning of 1975 the new model appeared on the market, called Mini 90 or 120: the 90 had the 998cc engine with 49bhp and the 120 the well-known 1275cc unit rated at 65bhp. The platform and subframes were the original Mini items and the new cars very soon became a favourite with the younger generation.

The Italian company, which had been acquired by Argentine Alejandro de Tomaso, as British Leyland closed down their own operation, launched a successor to the Mini Cooper at the 1976 Turin Salon. It had a more powerful 74bhp 1275cc engine, and was good for over 100mph. This top model from Milan with its black spoilers was available until 1982 – then this successor to the Innocenti Mini had a three-cylinder Daihatsu engine installed in its attractive exterior.

It may be estimated that the total production figure for all Innocenti Minis with the original body style from 1965 to 1976 was at least 400,000 cars, mostly sold in the Italian home market. These 'Italian Jobs' therefore made a substantial contribution to the overall production total of five million Minis world-wide, reached in 1986.

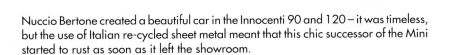

Nuccio Bertone created a beautiful car in the Innocenti 90 and 120 – it was timeless, but the use of Italian re-cycled sheet metal meant that this chic successor of the Mini started to rust as soon as it left the showroom.

MINIS in Miniature

Almost from the day of its introduction the Mini has been a popular subject with commercial model makers. Small reproductions have been produced in vast numbers as popular toys while at the other end of the scale – and at very much higher prices – there have been models for serious collectors and plastic of white-metal kits for serious modellers. Most of these have been to the accepted European scale of 1:43 and some allow for a kit to be completed in more than one standard form, for example as a normal road car or a rally car. Some of the models listed in the table are 'collectors' items' and change hands for serious money – these are not necessarily the earliest models, for some recent limited editions are already sought after.

Company	Country	Introduced	Type	Scale	Model number	Material
Airfix	Britain	1962	Morris Mini-Minor	1:32	M4C	Plastic kit
		-	Mini-Cooper	1:32	5095	Plastic
		-	Mini-Cooper	1:32	6067	Plastic kit
Anguplas	Spain	1962	Austin Seven Mini	1:86	65	Plastic
Asahi	Japan	-	Mini	1:43		Plastic
Burago	Italy	c.1979	Innocenti Mini 120	1:24		Metal
Carlo	Japan	-	Mini-Cooper S	1:43		Metal
Corgi Toys	Britain	1960	Morris Mini-Minor	1:43	226	Metal
		1961	Austin Seven Mini	1:43	225	Metal
		1962	Morris Mini-Cooper Competition (with flag decal on bonnet)	1:43	227	Metal
		1964	Mini-Cooper S, 1964 Monte Carlo rally winner	1:43	317	Metal
		1964	Austin Mini van	1:43	450	Metal
		1964	Police Mini van, with dog and handler	1:43	448	Metal
		1965	Mini Countryman, with surfer and board	1:43	485	Metal
		1965	Mini-Cooper S, 1965 Monte Carlo rally winner	1:43	321	Metal
		1965	Morris Mini-Cooper, with wickerwork	1:43	249	Metal
		1966	Mini-Cooper S, 1966 Monte Carlo rally car with signatures of Makinen and Easter on roof (same model number as 1965 car)	1:43	321	Metal
		1967	Mini-Cooper S, 1967 Monte Carlo rally winner	1:43	339	Metal
		1967	Mini-Cooper S, 1967 RAC Sun International rally car	1:43	333	Metal
		1967	Morris Mini-Mostest 'Pop-Art' (never officially released, but some in circulation)	1:43	349	Metal
		1968	Mini-Marcos, with Golden Jacks	1:43	341	Metal
		1968	Mini-Cooper 'Magnifique' with sunroof	1:43	334	Metal
		1971	Mini-Cooper rally car, white with Whizzwheels	1:43	282	Metal
		1971	London Gift Set – Mini, London bus and Taxi	1:43	11	Metal
		1972	Mini-Cooper Monte Carlo rally car, yellow with Whizzwheels	1:43	308	Metal
		1972	Morris Mini-Minor with Whizzwheels	1:43	204	Metal
		1972	Mini-Marcos with Whizzwheels	1:43	305	Metal
		1975	Minissima	1:36	288	Metal
		1976	Mini 1000 saloon	1:36	200	Metal
		1977	Mini Camping Gift Set	1:36	38	Metal
		1978	Mini 1000 saloon, racing version	1:36	201	Metal

In c.1984 the 1:36 Mini was deleted from the Corgi range but the model was re-introduced in 1989 on the initiative of the Rover Group, to serve as a memento of the Mini's 30th anniversary. The tooling was re-furbished and the model updated. The new Corgi Mini was first launched on the occasion of the Mini birthday party at Silverstone in August 1989.

		1989	30th Anniversary Mini, specially packaged for Rover, limited edition of 20,000 models of which 2500 with numbered certificates in special packaging together with Mini book	1:36		Metal
		1989	'Mini Racing' green	1:36		Metal
		1989	'Mini Flame' red	1:36		Metal
		1989	'Mini Sky'	1:36		Metal
		1989	'Mini Rose'	1:36		Metal
		1990	Mini Mayfair, blue or maroon	1:36		Metal
		1990	Mini City, yellow or silver	1:36		Metal

Company	Country	Introduced	Type	Scale	Model number	Material
		1990	Mini-Cooper, limited numbered edition of 6000 for Dixons, green	1:36		Metal
		1990	'Mini After Eight', special edition for Rover France, later released in the UK as standard model	1:36		Metal
		1990	Mini-Cooper, packaged for Rover, red with white roof and bonnet stripes, John Cooper signature	1:36		Metal
		1990	Set of three special edition models – Piccadilly, Park Lane and Chelsea – sold only in Woolworths ('Mini Racers' set)	1:36		Metal
		1991	Set of three special edition models – Red Hot, Jet Black and Ritz – sold only in Woolworths	1:36		Metal
		1992	'Mini Checkmate'	1:36		Metal
		1992	'Mini Neon'	1:36		Metal
		1992	'Mini Designer'	1:36		Metal
		1992	Mini-Cooper, no bonnet stripes or signature	1:36		Metal
		1992	1964 Monte Carlo winner, red/white	1:36		Metal
		1992	1960s John Cooper team racing Mini, green	1:36		Metal

The 1:36 scale Corgi Mini is still in production at the time of writing and there are likely to be further variants to come. There may have been additional variations of this model which are not listed here. In 1991 there was a new Corgi Mini model, as follows:

		1991	Mini, offer for tokens in a Kellogg's Corn Flakes promotion	1:50		Metal

For 1992, Corgi planned a revival of their old 1:43 scale Mini with a re-issue of some of the classic 1960s models:

		1992	Set of three Mini Monte Carlo winners (1964, 1965 and 1967)	1:43		Metal

It may also be mentioned that some Corgi Mini models of the 1960s were included in various Gift Sets, not listed here, but as far as is known these were always in standard liveries.

Company	Country	Introduced	Type	Scale	Model number	Material
Corgi Junior	Britain	1970	Mini-Cooper S, BVRT Vita-Min Hillclimb Champion	1:55	21	Metal
Daiya	Japan	-	Mini-Cooper, Monte Carlo rally car	1:12		Plastic
Diapet (Yonezawa)	Japan	-	Mini	1:35		Metal
Dickie	Japan	-	Mini	1:50		Plastic kit
Dinky Toys	Britain	1961	Morris Mini-Traveller	1:43	197	Metal
		1961	Austin Mini Countryman	1:43	199	Metal
		1964	Election Mini van, with figure and loudspeaker	1:43	492	Metal
		1964	Mini van, AA Service	1:43	274	Metal
		1965	Mini van, RAC Service	1:43	273	Metal
		1966	Military Mini-Moke, with parachute	1:43	601	Metal
		1966	Mini-Moke, civilian; with Speedwheels from c.1972 onwards	1:43	342	Metal
		1966	Morris Mini-Minor automatic (also Austin Mini-Cooper S); with Speedwheels from c.1972 onwards	1:40	183	Metal
		1967	Mini-Cooper S, Police car, with Speedwheels from c.1972 onwards	1:40	250	Metal
		1967	Stripey the Magic Mini, with four figures	1:40	107	Metal
		1967	'The Prisoner' Mini-Moke	1:43	106	Metal
		1970	Tiny's Mini-Moke, with giraffe driver	1:43	350	Metal
		1970	Mini van, 'Joseph Mason Paints' promotional	1:43	(274?)	Metal
		1975	Mini Clubman	1:40	178	Metal
		1977	Mini Clubman, Police car	1:40	255	Metal
Dinky Toys by Matchbox	Britain/China	1991	Austin Mini-Cooper S (white with black roof)	1:43	DY21	Metal

Other colour versions of this model are expected in 1993 and later.

Company	Country	Introduced	Type	Scale	Model number	Material
Eko	Spain	1968	Morris Mini-Minor	1:87	161 089	Plastic
Eligor	France	1985	Mini-Cooper S, 1965 Monte Carlo rally car	1:43	1111	Metal
		1985	Morris Mini-Minor 850	1:43	1110	Metal
		1985	Mini Parisienne	1:43	1113	Metal
		1985	Mini Police car	1:43	1112	Metal

The Eligor Mini models are based on the original Norev Mini of the 1960s, and all are still available at the time of writing.

Company	Country	Introduced	Type	Scale	Model number	Material
Graupner	Germany	-	Mini-Cooper (radio controlled model)	1:12		Kit

Company	Country	Introduced	Type	Scale	Model number	Material
GTM	Britain	-	Mini-Cooper	1:64		Metal kit
Guisval	Spain	-	Mini-Cooper	1:23		Metal
Heller	France	1975	Mini Special	1:43		Plastic kit
Hong Kong model	Hong Kong	-	Mini-Cooper	1:43		Metal
Imai	Japan	1979	Mini-Cooper S Mk II	1:20		Plastic kit
		1979	Innocenti Mini 120	1:20		Plastic kit
Jouef	France	-	Austin Mini-Cooper S	1:40	3550	Plastic
Joustra	Belgium/ Hong Kong	-	Mini	1:32	2587	Plastic
Kado	Japan	c.1980	Mini-Cooper S	1:43		Metal
Kawan	Japan	-	Innocenti Mini-Cooper	1:24		Plastic kit
L.S.	Japan	c.1980	Mini-Cooper S, 1968 Monte Carlo rally car	1:16		Plastic kit
		c.1980	Mini-Cooper S Mk II	1:16		Plastic kit
Matchbox	Britain	1971	Mini racing car with Superfast wheels	1:75	MB29	Metal
		1976	'Mini Ha-Ha', with fat rear wheels	1:75	MB14	Metal
		c.1979	Breakdown truck with Mini racing car (MB29)	1:75	TP6	Metal
Mattel	Italy	-	Innocenti Mini de Tomaso (ex-Mebetoys)	1:43	A108	Metal
Mebetoys	Italy	1968	Innocenti Mini-Minor	1:43	A28	Metal
		1969	Mini-Cooper rally car	1:43	A31	Metal
		1973	Innocenti Mini-Minor, with skis	1:43	A61	Metal
		1974	Innocenti Mini-Minor 'Hippy' (pop-art)	1:43	A71	Metal
		1976	Innocenti Mini 90	1:43	A86	Metal
		1978	Innocenti Mini de Tomaso	1:43	A108	Metal
		c.1976	Innocenti Mini 90	1:24		Metal
Mercury	Italy	1975	Innocenti Mini 90/120	1:43	20	Metal
		1975	Innocenti Mini 90/120, rally car	1:43	23	Metal
		1976	Innocenti Mini 90/120, with skis	1:43	24	Metal
Metosul	Portugal	1967	Morris Mini-Minor	1:43	7	Metal
			There have been several other variations on the Mini theme from Metosul.			
MRCC	Jersey	-	Austin/Morris Mini	1:32	5165	Plastic kit
Nacoral	Spain	c.1978	Morris Mini-Cooper	1:24	3501	Metal
		-	Mini-Cooper rally car	1:24	3551	Metal
		1973	Mini 1000	1:43	112	Metal
		1973	Mini 1000 rally car	1:43	112R	Metal
NET	?	-	Mini-Cooper with electric motor and remote steering by cable	1:17		Plastic
Norev	France	1963	Morris Mini-Minor 850 (also found in the cheap 'Baby' series without windows and interior)	1:43	75	Plastic
Pez	Italy	-	Innocenti Mini Mk II	1:36		Plastic
Pilen (Auto-Pilen)	Spain	1971	Mini-Cooper Mk III	1:43	319	Metal
		-	As above, but chrome-plated	1:43	320	Metal
		1975	Mini-Cooper rally car	1:43	291	Metal
Plasto	Finland	-	Mini	1:36		Plastic
Playart	Hong Kong	-	Mini-Cooper S (with trailer)	1:43	6000	Metal
Politoys/ Polistil	Italy	c.1970	Mini-Cooper S, Monte Carlo rally car	1:25	S582	Metal
		c.1972	Mini, Mato Grosso rally car	1:25	S628	Metal

Company	Country	Introduced	Type	Scale	Model number	Material
		c.1976	Mini rally car, 'Beaubourg' decor	1:25	S704	Metal
		c.1976	Innocenti Mini 1001	1:43	EL50	Metal
Scalextric	Britain	-	Mini-Cooper, front wheel drive	1:32	C76	Plastic
		-	Mini-Cooper, rear wheeel drive	1:32	C7	Plastic
		-	Mini-Cooper, rear wheel drive	1:32	C110/2	Plastic
		-	Mini Clubman, rear wheel drive	1:32	C122	Plastic
		-	Mini 'Mad Hatter' banger racer, rear wheel drive	1:32	C250	Plastic
		-	Mini 'Mini Ha-Ha' banger racer, rear wheel drive	1:32	C292	Plastic

All Scalextric models are slot racing cars.

Company	Country	Introduced	Type	Scale	Model number	Material
Scale Racing Cars	Britain	-	Mini-Cooper	1:43		Metal kit
SMTS	Britain	1990	Mini-Cooper S (road, racing or rally versions)	1:53	V3	Metal, kit or built up
Solido	France	1992	Mini-Cooper S	1:18		Metal

There are several different versions being planned of this model.

Company	Country	Introduced	Type	Scale	Model number	Material
South Eastern Finecast	Britain	1990	Austin/Morris Mini	1:43		Metal, kit or built up
		1990	Austin/Morris Mini-Cooper	1:43		Metal, kit or built up
Spot-On	N. Ireland	1962	Morris Mini Van, Royal Mail	1:42	210/1	Metal
		1962	Morris Mini Van, Post Office Telephones	1:42	210/2	Metal
		1962	Austin Mini saloon	1:42	211	Metal
		1966	Morris Mini Van, rear doors open, with figure	1:42	404	Metal
		1966	Morris Mini Van, as above less figure, 'Shell'	1:42	404/1	Metal
SRM	Britain	-	Mini-Cooper	1:40		Plastic
Tamiya	Japan	c.1985	Morris Mini-Cooper S Mk I 1275cc	1:24	39	Plastic kit
Technotoy	Japan	-	Mini-Cooper (radio controlled model)	1:18		Plastic
Thirty	Japan	-	Morris Mini-Traveller	1:43		Metal kit
Tomica	Japan	c.1981	Austin Mini Mk I, with Union Jack on roof	1:43	DF22	Metal
		c.1981	Mini-Cooper Monte Carlo rally car	1:43	DF26	Metal
		c.1981	Mini with two small motor cycles	1:43	DF27A	Metal
		c.1981	Mini with surfboard	1:43	DF27B	Metal
		c.1981	Mini with skis	1:43	DF27C	Metal
		c.1981	Mini 'Mountain Sports'	1:43	DF27D	Metal
Twin K-K	USA	-	Mini-Cooper	1:24		Plastic
Vitesse	Portugal	1991	Austin Mini-Cooper S	1:43	580	Metal
		1991	Morris Mini-Cooper S	1:43	581	Metal
		1991	Mini-Cooper S, 1964 Monte Carlo rally winner	1:43	582	Metal
		1991	Mini-Cooper, 1962 Monte Carlo rally car	1:43	SM76	Metal
		1991	Mini-Cooper, 1963 Monte Carlo rally car	1:43	SM77	Metal
		1991	Mini-Cooper S, 1965 Monte Carlo rally winner	1:43	SM78	Metal

Undoubtedly there are further versions being planned of the Vitesse Mini-Cooper. The non-rally versions are available in all the correct colour schemes for Austin/Morris Mini-Cooper Mark I cars.

Company	Country	Introduced	Type	Scale	Model number	Material
unknown	Hong Kong	c.1964	Wolseley Hornet	1:32		Plastic

Chrome-plated and friction driven but not too bad for all that – possibly the only model of the Hornet/Elf style to exist, although a white metal kit of the Hornet/Elf was being planned by a small British manufacturer in 1992.

This list of Mini models past and present is by no means complete, but it is hoped that the best-known and most popular models have all been included. The serious enthusiast for Mini models is recommended to study specialist publications which in Britain include 'Model Collector' magazine and others.

List compiled with assistance of, among others:
Bernd Schulz, die modellbox, Frankfurt a.M., Germany
Anders Ditlev Clausager; David Hodges;
Denis Chick, Rover Group External Affairs

Dinky Toys Moke with hood hoops in position.

Corgi Minissima.

Mini-Cooper S 1:24 kit by Tamiya.

Corgi Mini Monte Carlo in comtemporary setting.

Mini 1000 Camping Set by Corgi.

A fleet of Mnis. From left to right: Corgi Mini 1000, Corgi Mini Minor, Metosul Mni-Cooper, Corgi Mini with basketwork sides, Dinky Traveller.

Mini-Marcos 850GT by Corgi.

MINI Specifications

	Austin Seven/Mini Morris Mini-Minor (Austin/Morris 850) Mark I saloon	Austin Mini and Morris Mini-Minor Mark II 850 saloon	Austin Mini and Morris Mini-Minor Mark II 1000 saloon	Austin Seven/Mini Countryman and Morris Mini-Traveller Mark I	Austin Mini Countryman Morris Mini-Traveller Mark II 1000
Engine	4cyl, ohv, transverse				
Bore x stroke	62.9 x 68.3mm		64.6 x 76.2mm	62.9 x 68.3mm	64.6 x 76.2mm
Cubic capacity	848cc		998cc	848cc	998cc
Compression ratio	8.1:1 (automatic 9.0:1)		8.3:1 (automatic 8.9:1)	8.3:1	8.3:1 (automatic 8.9:1)
Power	34bhp @ 5500rpm (automatic 39.5bhp @ 5250rpm)		38bhp @ 5250rpm (automatic 41bhp @ 4850rpm)	34bhp @ 5500rpm	38bhp @ 5250rpm (automatic 41bhp @ 4850rpm)
Torque	44lb/ft @ 2900rpm (automatic 44lb/ft @ 2500rpm	45lb/ft @ 3450rpm	52lb/ft @ 2700rpm (automatic 52lb/ft @ 2400rpm)	44lb/ft @ 2900rpm	52lb/ft @ 2700rpm (automatic 52lb/ft @ 2400rpm)
Carburettor(s)	1 SU HS2 (automatic 1 SU HS4			1 SU HS2	1 SU HS2 (automatic 1 SU HS4)
Transmission	4-speed manual, fwd 4-speed automatic optional from 10/65	Manual: all-synchro from 9/68		Manual only	Manual: all-synchro from 9/68 Automatic optional
Chassis/body	Unitary construction with two subframes				
Suspension	Independent front/rear Rubber cones to 9/64 Hydrolastic from 9/64	Hydrolastic		Rubber cones	
Steering	Rack-and-pinion				
Brakes	Drums front and rear				
Length	120.25in/3054mm			129.9in/3299mm	129.5in/3289
Width	55in/1397mm	55.5in/1410mm			
Height	53in/1346mm			53.5in/1359mm	
Wheelbase	80.16in/2036mm			84.16in/2138mm	
Kerb weight	1380lbs/626kg	1400lbs/636kg		1428lbs/648kg	1503lbs/682kg
Top speed	72mph/116km/h (automatic 70mph)		75mph/121km/h	72mph/116km/h	75mph/121km/h
0-60mph	34secs (automatic 37secs)		22secs	36secs	22secs
Production period	5/59-10/67	10/67-12/69	10/67-12/69	9/60-10/67	10/67-10/69
Numbers produced (approximate)	Austin 435,500 Morris 510,000	Austin 154,000 (850 and 1000) Morris 206,000 (850 and 1000)		Austin 85,500 Morris 75,500	Austin 22,500 Morris 23,500

	Riley Elf and Wolseley Hornet Mark I	Riley Elf and Wolseley Hornet Mark II	Riley Elf and Wolseley Hornet Mark III	Austin/Morris Mini-Cooper 997cc	Austin/Morris Mini-Cooper 998cc
Engine	4cyl, ohv, transverse				
Bore x stroke	62.9 x 68.3mm	64.6 x 76.2mm		62.4 x 81.3mm	64.6 x 76.2mm
Cubic capacity	848cc	998cc		997cc	998cc
Compression ratio	8.3:1			9.0:1	
Power	37bhp @ 5500rpm	40bhp @ 5250rpm		55bhp @ 6000rpm	55bhp @ 5800rpm
Torque	45lb/ft @ 3450rpm	52lb/ft @ 2700rpm		54lb/ft @ 3600rpm	57lb/ft @ 3000rpm
Carburettor(s)	1 SU HS2			2 SU HS2	
Transmission	4-speed manual, fwd		All-synchro from 8/68 4-speed automatic optional from 10/67	Manual only	
Chassis/body	Unitary construction with two subframes				
Suspension	Independent front/rear Rubber cones	Rubber cones to 9/64 Hydrolastic from 9/64	Hydrolastic	Rubber cones	Rubber cones to 9/64 Hydrolastic from 9/64
Steering	Rack-and-pinion				
Brakes	Drums front and rear			Disc front, drum rear	
Length	128.75in/3270mm	130.31in/3310mm		120.25in/3054mm	
Width	55in/1397mm	55.5in/1410mm		55in/1397mm	
Height	53in/1346mm				
Wheelbase	80.16in/2036mm				
Kerb weight	1477lbs/670kg		1465lbs/665kg	1400lbs/636kg	
Top speed	72mph/116km/h	81mph/130km/h		85mph/137km/h	90mph/145km/h
0-60mph	36secs	27secs		19secs	17secs
Production period	10/61-11/62	2/63-10/66	10/66-8/69	8/61-1/64	1/64-10/67
Numbers produced (approximate)	Riley 3,522 Wolseley 3,166	Riley 17,816 Wolseley 16,785	Riley 9,574 Wolseley 8,504	Austin 12,600 Morris 12,600	Austin 18,000 Morris 23,500

	Austin/Morris Mini-Cooper Mark II	Austin/Morris Mini-Cooper S 1071cc	Austin/Morris Mini-Cooper S 970cc	Austin/Morris Mini-Cooper S 1275cc	Austin/Morris Mini-Cooper S 1275cc Mark II
Engine	4cyl, ohv, transverse				
Bore x stroke	64.6 x 76.2mm	70.6 x 68.3mm	70.6 x 61.9mm	70.6 x 81.3mm	
Cubic capacity	998cc	1071cc	970cc	1275cc	
Compression ratio	9.0:1		9.75:1	9.5:1	
Power	55bhp @ 5800rpm	70bhp @ 6000rpm	65bhp @ 6500rpm	76bhp @ 5800rpm	
Torque	57lb/ft @ 3000rpm	62lb/ft @ 4500rpm	55lb/ft @ 3500rpm	79lb/ft @ 3000rpm	
Carburettor(s)	2 SU HS2				
Transmission	4-speed manual, fwd All-synchro from 9/68	4-speed manual, fwd			All-synchro from 9/68
Chassis/body	Unitary construction with two subframes				
Suspension	Independent front/rear Hydrolastic	Rubber cones	Rubber cones to 9/64 Hydrolastic from 9/64		Hydrolastic
Steering	Rack-and-pinion				
Brakes	Disc front, drum rear	Disc front, drum rear Servo			
Length	120.25in/3054mm				
Width	55in/1397mm				
Height	53in/1346mm				
Wheelbase	80.16in/2036mm				
Kerb weight	1400lbs/636kg	1410lbs/640kg			
Top speed	90mph/145km/h	95mph/153km/h	97mph/156km/h		
0-60mph	17secs	11secs	11.8secs	10.6secs	
Production period	10/67-11/69	3/63-8/64	6/64-4/65	4/64-10/67	10/67-11/69
Numbers produced (approximate)	Austin 9,900 Morris 21,800	Austin 2,100 Morris 1,500	Austin 500 Morris 500	Austin 6,400 Morris 8,200	Austin 2,400 Morris 5,300

	Mini-Cooper S Mark III	Mini 850 saloon (850 City/Super from 7/79)	Mini 1000 saloon (1000 City/HL from 9/80)	Mini City E/HLE (Mayfair from 10/82, City from 10/88)	Mini Clubman 1000 saloon
Engine	4cyl, ohv, transverse				
Bore x stroke	70.6 x 81.3mm	62.9 x 68.3mm	64.6 x 76.2mm		
Cubic capacity	1275cc	848cc	998cc		
Compression ratio	9.75:1	8.3:1 (automatic 9.0:1)	8.3:1 (automatic 8.9:1)	10.3:1	8.3:1 (automatic 8.9:1)
Power	76bhp @ 6000rpm	34bhp @ 5500rpm (from 6/74 37bhp @ 5500rpm) (automatic 39bhp @ 5250rpm)	38bhp @ 5250rpm (from 6/74 40bhp @ 5100rpm) (automatic 41bhp @ 4850rpm)	40bhp @ 5000rpm (41PS DIN @ 5000rpm)	38bhp @ 5250rpm (from 6/74 40bhp @ 5100rpm (automatic 41bhp @ 4850rpm)
Torque	79lb/ft @ 3000rpm	44lb/ft @ 2900rpm (from 6/74 431lb/ft @ 2800rpm) (automatic 44.8lb/ft @ 2500rpm)	52lb/ft @ 2700rpm (from 6/74 51lb/ft @ 2600rpm) (automatic 52lb/ft @ 2750rpm)	50lb/ft @ 2500rpm (68NM @ 2500rpm)	52lb/ft @ 2700rpm (from 6/74 51lb/ft @ 2600rpm (automatic 52lb/ft @ 2750rpm)
Carburettor(s)	2 SU HS2	1 SU HS2 (from 6/74 1 SU HS4) (automatic 1 SU HS4)		1 SU HS4	1 SU HS2 (from 6/74 HS4) (automatic HS4)
Transmission	4-speed manual, fwd all-synchro	4-speed manual Automatic optional to 9/71	Automatic optional throughout		Manual to 10/75 Automatic opt. to 10/75 Auto. Only from 10/75
Chassis/body	Unitary construction with two subframes				
Suspension	Hydrolastic (last few cars may have had rubber cones	Rubber cones			Hydrolastic to 6/71 Rubber cones from 6/71
Steering	Rack-and-pinion				
Brakes	Drums front, drum rear Servo	Drums front and rear 2 circuits from 9/77		Front discs from 10/84 Servo from 10/88	Drums front and rear 2 circuits from 9/77
Length	120.25in/3054mm				124.6in/3165mm
Width	55in/1397mm	55.5in/1410mm			
Height	53in/1346mm			53.25in/1353mm from 10/84	53in/1346mm
Wheelbase	80.16in/2036mm				
Kerb weight	1525lbs/692kg	1360lbs/617kg		1380lbs/625kg City 1420lbs/645kg Mayfair	1406lbs/638kg
Top speed	97mph/156km/h	77mph/124km/h	82mph/132km/h	80mph/128km/h	74mph/119km/h
0-60mph	10.6secs	20.3secs	18.7secs	17.9secs	27secs
Production period	3/70-6/71	10/69-8/80	10/69-4/82	4/82 to date	10/69-8/80
Numbers produced (approximate)	1600 built-up in UK; estimated 18,000 CKD units for assembly abroad	407,670	1,437,116 (1970-end 1991 incl. City and Mayfair)	Included with Mini 1000, 1969-82	275,583 (incl. 1100 model)

	Mini Clubman 1100 saloon	Mini Clubman 1000 estate car (Mini 1000 HL estate from 8/80)	Mini Clubman 1100 estate car	Mini 1275GT	Mini 1100 Special (Mini 1300 Special)
Engine	4cyl, ohv, transverse				
Bore x stroke	64.6 x 83.7mm	64.6 x 76.2mm	64.6 x 83.7mm	70.6 x 81.3mm	64.6 x 83.7mm (70.6 x 81.3mm)
Cubic capacity	1098cc	998cc	1098cc	1275cc	1098cc (1275cc)
Compression ratio	8.5:1	8.3:1 (automatic 8.9:1)	8.5:1	8.8:1	8.5:1 (8.8:1)
Power	49bhp @ 5250rpm (45bhp DIN @ 5250rpm)	38bhp @ 5250rpm (from 6/74 40bhp @ 5100rpm) (automatic 41bhp @ 4850rpm)	49bhp @ 5250rpm (45bhp DIN @ 5250rpm)	60bhp @ 5250rpm (from 6/74 59bhp @ 5300rpm, 54bhp DIN @ 5250rpm)	45bhp DIN @ 5250rpm (54bhp DIN @ 5250rpm)
Torque	60lb/ft @ 2450rpm (55.7lb/ft DIN @ 2700rpm)	52lb/ft @ 2700rpm (from 6/74 51lb/ft @ 2600rpm) (automatic 52lb/ft @ 2750rpm)	60lb/ft @ 2450rpm (55.7lb/ft DIN @ 2700rpm)	69.5lb/ft @ 2500rpm (from 6/74 69lb/ft @ 3000rpm, 65.4lb/ft DIN @ 2500rpm)	55.7lb/ft DIN @ 2700rpm (65.4lb/ft DIN @ 2500rpm)
Carburettor(s)	1 SU HS4	1 SU HS2 (from 6/74 HS4) (automatic HS4)	1 SU HS4		
Transmission	Manual only	Manual to 10/75, and 8/80-2/82, auto. opt.; auto only 10/75-8/80	Manual only		
Chassis/body	Unitary construction with two subframes				
Suspension	Independent front/rear with rubber cones			Hydrolastic to 6/71 Rubber cones from 6/71	Rubber cones only
Steering	Rack-and-pinion				
Brakes	Drums front and rear 2 circuits from 9/77			Disc front, drum rear Servo; 2 circuits from 9/77	Drums front and rear 2 circuits
Length	124.6in/3165mm	133.9in/3401mm		124.6in/3165mm	120.25in/3054mm
Width	55.5in/1410mm				
Height	53in/1346mm	53.5in/1359mm		53in/1346mm; 53.55in/1360mm from 6/74	53in/1346mm
Wheelbase	80.16in/2036mm	84.16in/2138mm		80.16in/2036mm	
Kerb weight	1406lbs/638kg	1514lbs/687kg		1504lbs/683kg; from 6/74 1488lbs/675kg	1366lbs/620kg
Top speed	83mph/134km/h	74mph/119km/h	83mph/134km/h	87mph/140km/h	84mph/135km/h
0-60mph	17.9secs	27secs	17.9secs	13.7secs	16.6secs
Production period	10/75-8/80	10/69-2/82	10/75-8/80	10/69-8/80	1977-81
Numbers produced (approximate)	see Clubman 1000 saloon	197,606 (incl. 1100 model)	see Clubman 1000 estate car	110,673	73,753 (Belgian-built) 5100 (UK-built, 1979) 31,360 (1300 Special)

	New Mini-Cooper	ERA Mini Turbo	Austin/Morris Mini van/pick-up 850 (Mini 850 from 11/69) (Mini 95 from 1979)	Austin/Morris Mini van/pick-up 1000 (Mini 1000 from 11/69) (Mini 95 from 1979)	Austin/Morris Mini-Moke
Engine	4cyl, ohv, transverse				
Bore x stroke	70.6 x 81.3mm		62.9 x 68.3mm	64.6 x 76.2mm	62.9 x 68.3mm
Cubic capacity	1275cc		848cc	998cc	848cc
Compression ratio	9.75:1	9.4:1	8.3:1		
Power	61PS DIN @ 5550rpm	96PS DIN @ 6130rpm	34bhp @ 5500rpm; from 1974 33bhp @ 5300rpm	38bhp @ 5250rpm; from 1974 39bhp @ 4750rpm	34bhp @ 5500rpm
Torque	91NM DIN @ 3000rpm	115NM DIN @ 2650rpm	44lb/ft @ 2900rpm; from 1974 39.8lb/ft @ 2500rpm	52lb/ft @ 2700rpm; from 1974 51.5lb/ft @ 2000rpm	44lb/ft @ 2900rpm
Carburettor(s)	1 ARG/SU; from 10/91 fuel injection	1 ARG/SU, Garratt turbocharger	1 SU HS2 from 1974 1 SU HS4		1SU HS2
Transmission	4-speed manual, fwd all-synchro		4-speed manual, fwd all-synchro from1968		4-speed manual, fwd
Chassis/body	Unitary construction with two subframes				
Suspension	Independent front/rear with rubber cones				
Steering	Rack-and-pinion				
Brakes	Disc front, drum rear, servo, 2 circuits		Drums front and rear, 2 circuits from 1977		Drums front and rear
Length	120.25in/3054mm	120.5in/3060mm	van 129.9in/3299mm; pick-up to 1970 130.5in/3315mm, from 1970 130.2in/3307mm		120in/3048mm
Width	55.5in/1410mm				51.5in/1308mm
Height	53.25in/1353mm	52.4in/1331mm	Van to 1972 54.5in/1384mm; van from 1972 and all pick-ups 53.5in/1359mm		56in/1422mm
Wheelbase	80.1in/2035mm	80.2in/2037mm	84.16in/2138mm		80.16in/2036mm
Kerb weight	1530lbs/695kg	1624lbs/737kg	1960-69 van 1334lbs/606kg, pick-up 1328lbs/603kg; 1969-83 van 1371lbs/622kg, pick-up 1369lbs/621kg		1176lbs/534kg
Top speed	92mph/148km/h	110mph/177km/h	72mph/116km/h	75mph/121km/h	70mph/113km/h
0-60mph	11.2secs	7.8secs	34secs	22secs	32secs
Production period	7/90 to date	1989 to date	Van 1/60-5/83 Pick-up 2/61-10/80	10/67-5/83	10/64-10/68 (in UK)
Numbers produced (approximate)	25,879 to end 1991	377 to end 1991	Austin 1960-69; van 174,500;p;ick-up 18,000 Morris 1960-69; van 155,000; pick-up 13,500 Mini 1970-83; van: 850 94,899, 1000 82,356; pick-up: 850 12,130, 1000 15,397		Austin 5,422 Morris 9,096 (UK production only)

	Moke (Portuguese version)	Innocenti Mini-Minor Mark I saloon	Innocenti Mini-Minor Mark II/III saloon	Innocenti Mini-Matic saloon	Innocenti Mini-Cooper Mark I, II and III
Engine	4cyl, ohv, transverse				
Bore x stroke	64.6 x 76.2mm	62.9 x 68.3mm		64.6 x 76.2mm	
Cubic capacity	998cc	848cc		998cc	
Compression ratio	8.3:1	8.3:1 (9.0:1 from 1967)	9.0:1	8.9:1	9.0:1 (Mk II/III: 9.5:1)
Power	40PS DIN @ 4750rpm	37bhp @ 5500rpm (41.5bhp @ 5250rpm from 1967)	48bhp @ 5800rpm	46bhp @ 4800rpm	56bhp @ 5800rpm (Mk II/III: 60bhp @ 6000rpm)
Torque	68NM DIN @ 2500rpm	41.3lb/ft @ 2600rpm (47.4lb/ft @ 2500rpm from 1967)	47.6lb/ft @ 3000rpm	58.2lb/ft @ 2400rpm	57.9lb/ft @ 3000rpm (Mk II/III: 62lb/ft @ 3000rpm)
Carburettor(s)	1 SU HS4	1 SU HS2 (1 SU HS4 from 1967)	1 SU HS4		2 SU HS2
Transmission	4-speed manual, fwd all-synchro	4-speed manual, fwd	All-synchro on Mark III from 1970	4-speed automatic	4-speed manual, all-synchro from 1970
Chassis/body	Unitary construction with two subframes				
Suspension	Independent front/rear with rubber cones	Hydrolastic		Hydrolastic to 1972 Rubber cones from 1972	Hydrolastic
Steering	Rack-and-pinion				
Brakes	Disc front, drum rear, servo, 2 circuits	Drums front and rear			Disc front, drum rear servo
Length	127in/3226mm	120.28in/3055mm			
Width	56.75in/1441mm	55.5in/1410mm			
Height	57.5in/1461mm	52.75in/1340mm			
Wheelbase	80.16in/2036mm				
Kerb weight	1388lbs/630kg		1421lbs/645kg	1487lbs/675kg	1476lbs/670kg
Top speed	80mph/129km/h	78mph/125km/h	84mph/135km/h	78mph/125km/h	90mph/145km/h (Mk II/III: 93mph/150km/h)
0-60mph	28secs	29secs	27secs		15secs
Production period	1984-91	1965-68	1968-72	1970-76	1966-72
Numbers produced (approximate)	not available				

	Innocenti Mini t Mark I estate car	Innocenti Mini t Mark II/III estate car	Innocenti Mini t 1000 estate car	Innocenti Mini 1000/1001 saloon	Innocenti Mini-Cooper 1300 and 1300 Export
Engine	4cyl, ohv, transverse				
Bore x stroke	62.9 x 68.3mm		64.6 x 76.2mm		70.6 x 81.3mm
Cubic capacity	848cc		998cc		1275cc
Compression ratio	8.3:1(9.0:1 from 1967)	9.0:1			9.75:1
Power	37bhp @ 5500rpm (41.5bhp @ 5250rpm from 1967)	48bhp @ 5800rpm	55bhp @ 5600rpm		71bhp @ 5800rpm
Torque	41.3lb/ft @ 2600rpm (47.4lb/ft @ 2500rpm from 1967)	47.6lb/ft @ 3000rpm	56.4lb/ft @ 3200rpm		79.6lb/ft @ 3200rpm
Carburettor(s)	1 SU HS2 (1SU HS4 from 1967)	1 SU HS4			2 SU HS2
Transmission	4-speed manual, fwd	All-synchro on Mark III from 1970	All-synchro		
Chassis/body	Unitary construction with two subframes				
Suspension	Independent front/rear with rubber cones				
Steering	Rack-and-pinion				
Brakes	Drums front and rear				Disc front, drum rear, servo
Length	129.45in/3288mm	128.66in/3268mm	129.45in/3288mm	120.28in/3055mm	
Width	55.7in/1415mm			55.5in/1410mm	
Height	53.5in/1360mm			52.75in/1340mm	
Wheelbase	84.16in/2138mm			80.16in/2036mm	
Kerb weight	1454lbs/660kg	1520lbs/690kg	1586lbs/720kg	1487lbs/675kg	1520lbs/690kg
Top speed	74mph/119km/h	84mph/135km/h	89mph/144km/h	90mph/145km/h	98mph/157km/h
0-60mph	30secs	28.5secs	19secs		11.3secs
Production period	1966-68	1968-72	1972-76		1972-75
Numbers produced (approximate)	not available				